DESIGNS FOR A
HEALTHY HOME

DESIGNS FOR A
HEALTHY HOME

AN ECO-FRIENDLY APPROACH

DAN PHILLIPS

SOMA
san francisco

First published in 2000 by
HarperCollins*Illustrated*
an imprint of HarperCollins*Publishers,*
London, England

North American edition published 2002 by
SOMA Books by arrangement with
Carroll & Brown Limited.
SOMA Books is an imprint of
Bay/SOMA Publishing, Inc.
For information write
Bay/SOMA Publishing, Inc.,
444 De Haro Street,
San Francisco, CA 94107.

Text © 2000 Dan Phillips
Compilation © 2000 Carroll & Brown Limited
American Edition © 2002 Bay/SOMA
Publishing, Inc.

ISBN 1-57959-071-3

Library of Congress Cataloging-in-
Publication Data on file with the Publisher.

This book was originally conceived, designed
and produced by
Carroll & Brown Limited
20 Lonsdale Road
London NW6 6RD

Color reproduction by Colourscan
Printed and bound in Spain by Mondadori
with paper sourced from sustainable forests

D.L. TO: 332-2002

This book is typeset in Rotis

Distributed by Publishers Group West

Contents

Eco-principles

Many ecological home design books recommend that the only way forward is to move out of the city and build a self-sufficient retreat away from the madding crowd. No matter how appealing this idea may seem, few of us have the desire or the practical ability to start again. The reality is that urban living is here to stay, so we should all try to discover how we can move toward a more ecologically sympathetic and caring home life, wherever it is we live.

Chapter One

Why eco-friendly?

Our homes protect us from the weather and provide us with a space where good memories and experiences can grow. With a little extra thought on our part, they can also connect us with the pleasures of the natural world, keeping us in touch with the seasons and providing our families with a buffer against some of the frustrations of our fast and modern lives. Our homes also reflect ourselves, so it's equally important that we find a way of living that is comfortable and compatible with our personal outlook on life.

But why choose eco-friendly alternatives when you can surely do all these things without worrying too much about the consequences? The reasons are simple enough: eco-friendly homes are cleaner, more cost-effective and more fun. They consume less, do more, last longer, support your local community and help you to connect with the outside world.

On a broader level, we are now faced with the need to improve the quality of our home environment, perhaps more so than in any other time in our history. In the past two hundred years, the world's population has increased from 1 billion to 6 billion, and we have changed from mainly pastoral and sedentary beings to fast-living urban dwellers who travel frequently—and often globally.

We also consume vast quantities of fuel and materials, creating pollution and waste on an unprecedented scale.

Our homes, innocent though they may seem, are responsible for over half of all this consumption and also harbor the causes of many modern ailments. These are two clear reasons for carefully considering the choices we make for our homes.

WHAT MAKES AN ECO-FRIENDLY HOME?

Ecology is the study of how living creatures interact with each other and the natural world, while friendliness is a state of mind that puts care and good humor at the top of the agenda. Eco-friendly homes can therefore be defined as homes that are kind to the environment, to our families and to the people around us, both around the corner and around the globe.

< express yourself

Your home should reflect your personality, so don't restrict your individual style—anything from kitsch to classic can be considered eco-friendly. Aim to strike a balance so that you can enjoy your immediate surroundings and care for the environment in the long term as well.

More specifically, an eco-friendly home is one that is made from nontoxic materials that are easy to reuse or recycle; contains long-lasting, well-made and multifunctional furniture and fixtures; uses energy economically so that it is efficient and cheap to run; is designed with the natural elements in mind so its interiors are connected with the outside, natural world; blends in well with your local community; and, finally, has a sense of fun and comfort to it.

Instead of simply allowing it to be "a machine for living in," try to make your home funky and tough. Break down the barriers between rooms, understand the surfaces and furniture in your home and enjoy them. Choose items that are multifunctional and adaptable: a table on wheels that splits in two can be used for writing, dining and even as a plaything for the kids. A child's cot can turn into a chair and a climbing frame. As well as being comfortable and attractive, every item in an eco-friendly home should work and play hard too.

But do we have to live like eco-warriors to be eco-friendly? Of course not! Simple measures, such as changing a standard lightbulb to a fluorescent one, will make the lighting in your home last ten times longer. Using gas heating instead of electric will cut your energy bills, while installing proper controls and insulating your windows will further reduce your home's energy consumption. Choosing wood flooring instead of wall-to-wall carpets will not only reduce your housecleaning work but will also allow your floor to last a lifetime. All it takes is a little knowledge and forethought.

∧ hardworking homes

Our homes should be flexible and fun, inspiring us to enjoy the world around us, and be able to adapt to our constantly changing needs. They should provide a calming environment in which we can either relax and be alone, or entertain and be sociable. Our homes should protect us against the elements and pollution of all kinds, and yet connect us with the world outside.

The key concepts

Eco-friendly living encapsulates both basic and eclectic ideas. Some, such as recycling, are familiar and frequently practiced in many homes. Others, such as choosing renewable sources of energy, may be less common. To start with, adopt the ones that suit you most, then explore the others as time goes by.

SUPPORT YOUR LOCAL COMMUNITY

No one is an island and the choices we make all have an effect on others and the planet. Being aware of this will help us to ensure that our actions help rather than harm. One way to do this is to find local people to maintain your home and choose locally made products to furnish it. This benefits everyone by keeping cash in your community and providing common ground. It also avoids the transportation costs, energy and pollution that result from buying from afar. If you do buy products from distant communities, always pay a fair price for fair trade. Never buy products that have been made on the back of someone else's poverty. As the saying goes, "think globally, but act locally."

Think about ways of improving your community too. A tree-lined street with clean pavements and local shops will improve the quality of your life and add value to your home. Instead of complaining, think of ways to make your neighborhood a cleaner, friendlier and safer place. Petition your city council to slow down traffic, hold a fête in the street to raise money for local kids, or even invite your neighbors for a picnic in the local park!

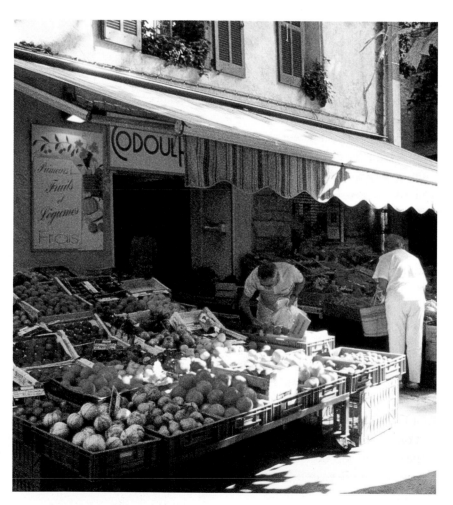

∧ fresh and local
Using your local greengrocer or market in preference to out-of-town shopping centers will not only keep cash in your community, it will also help to improve the quality of your local neighborhood.

SMALL IS BEAUTIFUL

Living simply often means doing more with less. Big and unwieldy homes are a bit like large, high-powered cars. They are invariably far harder to look after than smaller versions. Just like the Mini Moke or the Fiat 500, smaller homes are easier to handle and personalize. But choosing small things doesn't mean rejecting quality. Like a vase or a handcrafted sculpture, a small home can be an object of beauty too. As the German-born architect Mies van der Rohe said, "God is in the details."

RENEWABLE POWER

Of all the choices that we can make, the key to conserving resources is to find ways of making the need for power stations and diesel-guzzling trucks vanish. When you take out a normal lightbulb and replace it with a compact fluorescent one, you reduce the electricity needed by 80 percent; with enough flourescent bulbs, a power station will eventually disappear. When you replace a south-facing single-glazed window with a high-efficiency double-glazed unit, the window captures more heat from the sun than it loses, becoming a natural heater. When you buy a secondhand mahogany table from the corner shop or hand one down to your children, a tree in Malaysia will not be chopped down, a forest may not be destroyed, a truck will not cross the country and a motorway may not be built.

Conserving energy and using renewable power needn't be a chore or a burden. In the not-too-distant future, we may all be installing our own miniature power stations in our homes or local communities. Many experts predict that we will be purchasing micro fuel cells that can generate electricity by chemical reaction. These will run on ethanol (which is produced from crops like sugar cane) and their only waste product will be water.

Until this happens, there are plenty of other renewable energy technologies that use the sun or the wind to harness natural energy sources. The simplest and most widely available renewable energy source is wood. Trees also absorb carbon dioxide and air pollution, and they help to improve the quality of cities and the countryside. Growing trees is therefore a small but important part of sustainable living.

alternative energy
Wind turbines (below) and solar photovoltaic tiles (right) are just two forms of renewable power now available. Even using sunshine instead of artificial lighting will encourage environmental protection.

Photovoltaic systems are now available that can make any existing home into a net exporter of electricity. While these systems are uncommon and still expensive, it is likely that prices will fall and numbers will increase as manufacturers develop the technology.

Wind turbines are a common sight in windy rural locations where the costs of installing

ECO-TIP

Eco-friendly electricity
Your home's electrical supply comes from a power station far away. It's easy to think that you can't control the way a supplier maintains their plant and how that affects your environment. Yet it is possible to choose your electricity from a company that delivers renewable electricity direct to your home. This reduces the need for companies to build new power stations, as well as the pollution caused by the burning of fossil fuels. Future changes in technology will create even greater energy savings as lights and appliances will turn on only when they are needed and turn off automatically when you leave the room. Until then, do the planet a favor and switch off lights and heaters when they're not really needed.

electrical cables or oil-fueled generators are high. Economies of scale suggest wind turbines will probably develop into a major source of large-scale energy generation rather than be used as household items, but remote communities may find that they are actually a good solution for their electrical needs.

Even if you don't install high-technology solutions, it's good to remember that simply opening a window for summer ventilation or installing a skylight for daylight means that you are part of the renewable energy community and are helping to reduce dependency on fossil fuels.

SUSTAINABLE MATERIALS

The style, materials and color of your personal possessions mark out your own tastes, while their cracks, chips and grime give you a clue as to how well your choices have stood the test of time.

Look around your home to see what furniture is working well and where the chips and cracks are appearing. You will soon discover that solid timber furniture can be dented and knocked and still retain a certain pride, while laminated surfaces chip easily at corners, exposing rough and ugly MDF. Cast-iron pots last well compared to the slicker aluminum pans with nonstick finishes that always seem to fail eventually. Plastic electrical sockets gather grime and you'll wish you forked out that little extra for chrome or brass fittings.

Look continually, not only at the surface of your possessions but also at their depth and flexibility.

LIVING THE THREE RS

The ecological mantra "reduce, reuse, recycle" describes a set of ideas that help you to conserve resources in your home and to decrease the mounting piles of waste being dumped in landfill sites around the world every day. Nature works in a cycle so that waste becomes food for other living systems, and we should try to do the same in our homes.

Reduce
To limit your material consumption and therefore decrease the strain on the world's resources, choose products that are long lasting and have minimal packaging. Buy in bulk and borrow or rent occasional items rather than buying them (the average household drill is said to be used for only half an hour in its lifetime). Renting a car will save money and energy, while giving you the choice of vehicle depending on your need, for example, a van for collecting furniture or a small car for visiting family and friends. In fact, it won't be long before companies that used to sell fridges will be selling a year's worth of cooling, recycling components when your fridge needs to be repaired and installing more efficient parts when they become available.

Reuse

Get into the reusing swing by purchasing high-quality second-hand furniture. Repair appliances and furniture rather than throwing them away. Keep a strong plastic or canvas bag and use this for grocery shopping instead of using the countless flimsy bags supplied by most supermarkets. Use washable plates and cutlery for picnics and outings instead of

hope house

The English architect Bill Dunster has designed an attractive and eco-friendly home and work space. Its key features include the south-facing, triple-story glazed atrium that stores heat, the mono-pitched metallic roof and the weather-board upper stories, providing light, air and lots of warmth.

< long lasting
Sustainable materials, such as wood and clay, are safe, plentiful and long lasting. Used creatively, they not only make beautiful and practical furniture and fittings but also age well.

plastic disposable ones. Cut up old plastic bottles and use them in the garden to protect growing plants. Replace the covers on a worn sofa or, if you've had enough of it, give it to a charity or a used-furniture shop where it will find a second home.

Recycle
Finally, choose items that can easily be recycled or upgraded when they come to the end of their lives. Buy solid monolithic furniture that can be dismantled and recycled once you have finished with it. This reduces landfill waste and the need to dig up more metals from the earth, cut down more forests or synthesize more oil to make plastics.

One way to encourage recycling is to buy products with recycled components. These range from recycled office paper to terrazzo floor tiles made from old wine bottles.

LIVING WITH THE SEASONS
Nowadays, we often wear T-shirts in winter and work in artificially lit and air-conditioned offices and shops in summer. When our lives are dominated by artificial environments it's easy to lose touch with the changing seasons, and even the line between day and night can become blurred.

Rather than accepting this, design your home so that you live your life in tune with the seasons. Eat fresh salads and berries in summer and vegetable stews in winter. If you have the space, build an unheated lean-to greenhouse and use it for growing plants in spring and as an extra room in warmer weather. Go out in the garden or a park during warm seasons and, when winter comes, snuggle up together with family and friends. All these things will not only create a more active and varied home experience but will also save energy and resources.

CREATING GREEN SPACE
Our cities are covered in asphalt and concrete, and our lives are overwhelmed by electronics and artificial media. Often the only plants we see are imported cut flowers and bedraggled street trees fighting off smog. Creating green space is one way to combat this urban shock and give something back to nature. A garden, balcony or any outdoor space is worth its weight in gold in our crowded cities and we should use them to encourage flora and fauna. Equally, keeping plants inside our homes will help to clean the air and provide color and perfume.

Gardening shouldn't be seen as a battle against nature and disorder but as a search for balance between the weather, the soil, flora and fauna. If you make a careful initial selection of the plants, they will require no more than pruning and occasional weeding. The resulting wildflowers, trees and hedges will provide a varied environment of sun, shade and shelter at different scales. Plants that will grow successfully depend on the garden climate, the quality of the underlying soil and how much time you have for caring for them.

WHAT NEXT?

Many people and organizations are providing inspiring ways to improve our relationships with each other and the natural world, and I hope this book does the same. Chapter 2, Essential Elements, examines the location and structure of your home, and it explores how you can use light,

> **garden gorgeous**
This potential ecological resource improves the local climate, enriches the soil, encourages birds and insects to live and can provide you with seasonal fruits and vegetables.

color and texture efficiently and creatively. In addition, it explains how to maintain healthy air and water and gives advice on choosing energy-efficient and safe systems for heating, cooling and powering your home.

Chapter 3, Eco-Materials, considers the environmental credentials of the materials used to build and furnish homes, explaining why materials matter, both locally (for your own health and comfort) and globally (for the planet and distant communities).

Chapter 4, Rooms for Living, looks at all the areas of your home and how you can improve them, no matter what your style or budget, while chapter 5, People and Pets, looks at changing your home to accommodate the changing lives of its inhabitants.

Chapter 6, Upkeep, looks at how we can maintain and clean our homes without damaging the earth, while chapter 7, The Eco-Rating Guide, provides an overall eco-score for many of the materials and products found in the book.

I hope *Designs for a Healthy Home* provides a clear understanding of how you can make positive choices in and around your home to encourage a sustainable future. Just as important, I hope you enjoy the book and your homes.

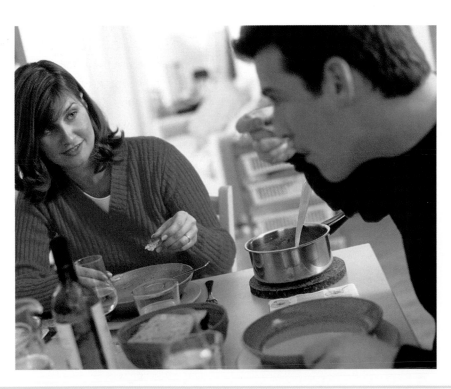

< **warm and cozy**
Instead of turning up the heat on cold days, wear a sweater, drink a cup of hot soup or go for a run!

Essential elements

"There is a circle of questions with a very large circumference and no centre. And what all these questions come to is, 'how am I to live?'" (Robert Musil, *The Man Without Qualities*, vol. 3 [London: Secker & Warburg, 1979])

The possibilities for choosing where to live and how to renovate your home are endless. Whether you live in a hot or cold climate, are old or young, are buying somewhere new or old, are renovating your home from top to bottom or are simply needing to rejuvenate one or two rooms, this chapter advises you on the essential elements of your home, helping you to fill in your own circle.

Surveying your home

If you are considering moving to a new home, you are in the fortunate position of being able to find somewhere with good eco-credentials. Real estate agents might insist there are just three factors to choosing a home—location, location and location—but, while property moguls espouse zip codes, we really should champion fresh air, clean water and natural light, as well as protection from the elements and a connection with the rhythms of the natural world. Your new home must also fit into your real life, being part of a valuable community, close to friends and family, and near work and play.

The key to finding this ideal eco-home is to look for a well-designed building that sits comfortably in its surroundings, away from noise and pollution. It should make the most of the sun in winter and be sheltered from strong winds (and do the opposite in hot climates). There should be good views from the windows, but also some privacy from neighbors. Make sure the ground on which it is built drains well, the building structure itself is sound and well insulated against noise and the weather, and there is enough space for all your needs.

Not all these criteria are visible to the untrained eye, so you may need a good inspector (preferably one sympathetic to eco-principles) who can draw up a detailed report on the building before you commit yourself to buying.

While you can do little about your location if you're already settled in your home, there are still plenty of modifications you can make, both to your home and to how you use it. These vary in scale from the major, such as building a conservatory or installing solar panels, to the minor, such as buying low-energy bulbs and fitting weather stripping to door and window frames. Each adds, often invisibly, to the comfort and quality of your home.

< eco-elements
Sometimes it is obvious from the outside that a house has eco-friendly elements. At other times, you will need to examine its structure and surroundings more carefully to confirm this.

FACTORS TO CONSIDER

The table below provides a list of factors that can affect your home. Consider these when assessing the eco-worthiness of your home—be it old or new.

	Positive factors	Negative factors
Location	Quiet, unpolluted street	Noise and pollution from nearby roads or neighbor
	Close to green space	Urban jungle
	Multicultural	Monocultural
	Close to work, shops and leisure activities	Under electrical high-voltage towers or near sub-stations
	Personal outside space	No external space
	Tree-lined streets	Area affected by radon
	Good views	Shadows from surrounding buildings
	No light pollution at night	Badly designed street lights near the house
Structure	Sound	Problematic
	Airtight	Leaky doors, windows and walls
	Damp-proof	Musty air (a sign of damp penetration)
	Well-insulated roof and walls (cavity construction with insulation)	Solid wall construction with no insulation
	Double glazing	Single glazing
	Good ventilation (windows opening onto clean streets)	Poor ventilation (few openable windows and those that do face stagnant spaces)
	All rooms with good natural light and high ceilings	Poor sunlight penetration (surrounded by tall buildings)
	Southern (sun-facing) or western aspect (in cool climates) or shaded aspect (in warm climates)	
	Just big enough	Too large or too small
Services	Efficient gas heating (in town) or high-efficiency wood-fired stove (in country)	Electric or oil heating
	Clean, newer water pipes and tanks	Old galvanized-steel pipes or broken drains

Making
space

While materials, color, light and texture define the surfaces of our homes, it is the space between the walls that holds the key to living well. To get a real feel for this space you need to live in it for a while. So, if you have moved to a new home, don't rush into instant renovations. Instead, do nothing for a while and simply watch how the space in each room changes throughout the day and the seasons. Scribble down notes and ideas, then discuss them with your partner, friends or other members of your household.

While you are doing this, set about correcting or improving the basics. This may include fixing structural defects, rewiring, replumbing, and sealing and insulating the building.

If the existing decorations are too much for your tastes, make some simple adjustments. Pull up old and dirty carpets (you may even be able to recycle them by giving them to a charity rather than throwing them away), or whitewash the walls and ceilings.

ALLOCATING ROOMS
Rooms are best laid out to harmonize with nature and any unchangeable man-made conditions. If you have the luxury of influencing the design of your

> take it slowly
If it is possible, keep some of your furniture in storage while you grow into your new home. Only then will the space between the walls trickle out and give you clues as to how you can proceed.

new home, or you can assign rooms to face specific directions, the first thing to consider is the time that you use each room and where the sun is in relation to the room throughout the day and the year (see chart opposite). Other factors, such as the amount of noise and pollution each room receives from the street, whether there is a lot of shade from trees or neighboring buildings, and what the view is like, also need consideration if the layout of your home is to work well.

A sunny disposition
Rooms warmed by the sun are more comfortable and require less heating, so use them as living or working spaces. Rooms that aren't should be reserved for bathrooms and storage space. In warmer climates practice the opposite.

Upstairs or downstairs?
While there may be practical reasons to keep common rooms at ground level and place private

rooms above, doing so will not necessarily create the most inspiring plan. Since we spend more waking hours in our living rooms, the quality of natural light and the views these rooms have are more critical. Often the best place to gain these benefits is on the upper floors.

Equally, bedrooms are generally more contemplative spaces that need less light, so they can therefore be sited on the lower floors. What's more, living rooms need to be warmer than bedrooms and, because warm air rises, the upper rooms are often warmer than ground floor spaces. Smells will also rise, so situating the kitchen on the top floor is a good idea since it is less likely to fill your home with the aroma of your last meal.

IDEAL ROOM LOCATIONS

The sun and wind have always been dominating influences on the home—cave dwellings were chosen to catch the sun in cold climates, while homes in the tropics were built with wide verandas to shade them from sun and raised on stilts to catch breezes. Sunshine is a real mood booster, so make the most of it when planning your home. Below is a list of ideal room locations if you live in the northern hemisphere.

Room	Location
Bedrooms	Facing northeast to southeast so they catch the rising sun.
Kitchens and workrooms	Southeast to southwest so they stay bright and airy in the day. If southern space is cramped, they can also be located to the north since these rooms often produce their own heat.
Living and dining rooms	South to northwest so they are washed by the evening sun.
Gardens	Facing southeast to west so they are sunny in the afternoon and early evening.
Halls and utility rooms	Facing north to act as a buffer against the cold in winter.
Bathrooms	East for morning people and west for evening people.

External noise

Noise and pollution from the street can spoil the overall harmony of your home, so less social rooms, such as the bathroom, should face the street. Make sure any windows in rooms that face a main road or busy street can be kept closed. Planting hedges and trees or building small utility spaces between your home and the road will help. If none of this is possible, then you'll have to deal with the noise by installing

> sound barriers

Tall plants and bushes will keep your garden private, shielding it from the gaze of curious onlookers. A living willow like this will also help to block out any noise and absorb pollution from nearby roads.

secondary window glazing. This will help to insulate your home in winter, but lack of ventilation can also make it overheat in summer.

Shade from adjacent buildings often cuts out sunlight, even in south-facing rooms. If this is the case with your home, paint the rooms a light color to make the most of the reduced natural light, and create warmth internally through the use of rich colors in furniture and fixtures. You may even be able to create a skylight in the roof to brighten upper rooms.

CREATING MORE SPACE

Many homes were built for a completely different age, with rooms designed to suit different needs and different people. For example, many homes built in the nineteenth century were designed for large families who stayed together over a number of generations. This often led to houses with many small rooms, each functioning according to the cultural mores of that time. The kitchen was often small and separated from the dining room. There was frequently a playroom for the children and another for the adults, a room for special occasions and one for day-to-day use. Basements and upper floors were given far less height and partitioned off to become servants' quarters or bedrooms for the household's youngest children.

Many of these houses have now been converted into flats by developers who have installed even more partitions to create more rooms. One way to free up the potential of homes like these is to knock down walls. Corridors and lobbies can become usable spaces, and light from the sunny side of your home can penetrate through to the areas of your home that are dark or shadowed. Rooms that once supported only one function can suddenly become multifunctional and fun.

Seeing this potential may take a little time and may also require some serious investigation and expense on your part, but it can often result in a valuable addition to your home. Before you take down a wall, however, make sure you consult an architect or engineer (see page 65, chapter 3).

Extensions

If you lack space, consider an extension to your home, since this is often much cheaper than moving to a larger home. If you have a garage, park the car on the street and convert this room into a workshop. Alternatively, add some windows and good insulation to make it a study or spare bedroom. As well as adding value, major changes like these are excellent opportunities to improve the overall efficiency of your home.

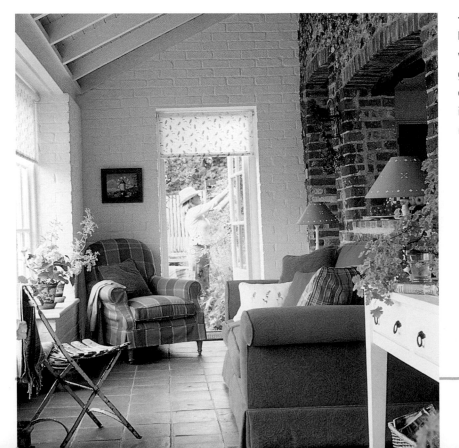

< creating a sunroom
If your home has a veranda, enclose it with windows to create a sunroom. The glass will capture the sun's heat and create a naturally warm space. This room is also good for growing plants year-round, bringing you closer to nature.

> opening up the roof
Create more space by installing skylights and insulation in the attic. With an external balcony, this room can have the best views in the whole house.

Expanding into the garden

The father of British build-it-yourself housing design,
Walter Segal, built his first timber-framed house at the end
of his garden. Many local authorities allow you to build a
small detached building within your garden without the
need for planning approval, and it is often far easier and
cheaper to build a small, self-contained garden building
than it is to adapt your existing structure. This eco-friendly
retreat at the bottom of a north London garden was
designed by the architect Sarah Wigglesworth.

Letting the
light in

Light defines space, so it is important to understand how we can bring more natural light into our homes and use artificial light more creatively and economically. It is also important to understand how color can complement light sources and subsequently the qualities of each room in your house.

The sun is the most efficient light source we have, yet we are no longer solely creatures of the day, so artificial light is just as important as natural light. Balancing the transparency and clarity of natural light with the subtle qualities of well-designed artificial lighting will create a home that works day and night, throughout the year.

SUNLIGHT

Economically, ecologically, emotionally and aesthetically, it is far better to use natural light throughout your home. Apart from the obvious fact that it is free and wastes no electricity, exposure to the sun has a positive effect on your emotional well-being. Abundant windows are the best way to spread daylight through your home. However, it's important to bear in mind that although huge windows may create bright homes, they also let the heat in and out, which means you may need a huge furnace to keep warm in the winter and an

> **rays of sunshine**
On a sunny day, aim to let as much natural light into your home as possible. White walls and polished floors reflect light, brightening the room even further.

air-conditioning system to keep cool in the summer.

Skylights are one good way to let sunlight into your home. These small roof-mounted windows can fill your entire hallway with light if placed at the top of a staircase. Light-pipe skylights are also worth considering. These stainless-steel pipes funnel daylight deep into the center of your home from glazed dome inlets on the roof and are particularly good for brightening up internal rooms. Simpler ways to bring more natural light into your home include using aluminum venetian blinds on windows, which can bounce light deep into a room. Fixing curtain rails to extend beyond the edge of the window and allow you to draw back the curtains fully will also make a difference in the amount of sunshine a room receives. Even decorating with light colors will brighten your home and reduce the need for artificial lights during the daytime.

ELECTRIC LIGHTING

The ability to transform space with the flick of a switch is one of the wonders of modern times, yet many lighting designers take this for granted and care little about the energy needed to reproduce the sun's stunning light effects. In an eco-friendly home, you have to try a little harder, so that light follows function and form and you are using efficient sources of light.

Suiting the mood

Rooms should be lit according to the task at hand, so make sure workrooms, kitchens and studies have more light than rooms used for relaxing, such as bedrooms and living rooms. Also, rooms do not need to be washed in an even light, so use lights in particular areas for specific purposes: a bedside light for reading, a desk lamp for studying or an under-cabinet light for food preparation. These pools of light not only allow you to work while your family relax but also create an ambience that is far more pleasant

TECHNOLOGY

fluorescent bulbs

These use less than a fifth of the energy needed by a standard tungsten bulb and last up to ten times longer. Electricity passes through the electrodes at each end of the sealed fluorescent tube, which contains mercury vapor in an argon gas. This generates electrons, which form an arc that knocks electrons in the mercury atoms out of their normal position. When the electrons return to their normal position, they produce ultraviolet (UV) light. These UV rays strike phosphor particles, coating the wall of the tube and creating a fluorescent glow.

electrode generating electric charge

electron

mercury atom generating an arc

phosphor particles

light

UV rays from electron

than the general glow from a single ceiling fixture.

Also, as the Japanese writer Tanizaki advocated in his book *In Praise of Shadows,* the mystery and depth of shadow is just as important as light in a suitable atmosphere. So, where possible, choose lamps that allow you to alter the direction of light to suit your needs. A well-designed desk lamp can be pointed over your head for reading or twisted around to wash the wall and create a background glow.

Diffuse light is more relaxing to the eye than a single bulb, so use a translucent lamp shade or throw light up onto the ceiling or onto a wall. Uplights need more power than downlights and should only be used as low-voltage background lighting in combination with other local sources of light.

Energy-efficient lights

Ninety percent of all household electric lights use standard tungsten bulbs. These consume a quarter of all the electricity needed in the home, yet they produce nine times more heat than light, making them little more than inefficient electric heaters that also happen to glow a little. What's more, they only last a thousand hours before burning out. Luckily, there are plenty of alternatives that are just as attractive, last far longer and use less energy.

∧ lighting in situ

This living space has several types of lighting for optimum adaptability. Skylights (with external blinds) allow natural light into the room, while downlights create ambience. Spotlights illuminate pictures to their best advantage and table lamps provide pools of light by each sofa. To save energy, always turn lights off when they are not needed.

< lighting options

LIGHTING EFFICIENCY SCALE

Below is a comparative list of the efficiency, duration and running cost of various home lighting options. (It's all over for the standard lightbulb!)

Light source	Efficiency	Life (hours)	Running cost each year
Daylight	100%	Forever	Zero
Fluorescent	20%	10,000	Low
Halogen	8%	5,000	Medium
Standard tungsten	4%	1,000	High

Ceiling lights are the most efficient form of light because they throw light directly at you, but they only work well if they are directly over the area of activity at hand. A light that hangs low over the dining table is good, but one that sits in the middle of the room over nothing in particular won't be very useful or efficient.

The best lighting options are compact and linear fluorescent bulbs (see page 26). Unlike older versions, which flickered for a few seconds before coming on, modern compact fluorescent bulbs start almost instantaneously and have

A table lamp (top) not only provides a soft, sympathetic light but also adds a decorative element to a room. A string of recycled television screens (middle) creates a modern installation, while colored wall washers (below) bathe textured walls in a gentle ambient glow.

color rendering similar to tungsten bulbs so that they generate a warmer light instead of the traditional cool light that was thought to cause headaches. And you can now buy linear tubes with dimmers.

If you want to light a single object, such as your favorite painting, 12-volt halogen bulbs are good alternatives. These have a very white, punchy light and are twice as efficient as tungsten bulbs. They can be bought with integral transformers as well as wire tracks, which allow you to install them without having to take down the ceiling.

By switching to fluorescent or halogen lights, you will not only create a more attractive and varied home but also reduce your electricity bill by about a fifth, prevent the manufacture of around 150 normal bulbs and reduce carbon dioxide output from power stations by around 1,500 kg a year.

Encouraging clean air

Invisible and all around us, air fills our home, carrying sound, smell, pollution and fire. If you encourage the positive aspects of air and banish the negative, not only will your home smell cleaner, but you will also feel healthier too.

A good source of fresh air is vital for our well-being. The air inside our homes will only ever be as good as the air outside and is often far worse. When you walk in from the street, your shoes bring with them dirt and grime. In fact, according to the World Resource Institute, 95 percent of the lead and pesticides found in our homes comes in on our shoes.

AVOIDING AIR POLLUTION

One way of filtering outside air is to grow a leafy hedge between the street and your home. This will absorb some of the pollution and act as a noise barrier. The best approach, however, is to start a no-shoes policy at home. Put a shoe rack by your front door and provide socks and slippers for guests. This may take time to become a habit, but it will cut down on your cleaning time and definitely be worth it in the end.

Since pollution is worse by roads, always try to open windows that are facing away from the main road. Air from the back of the home may not be clean, but it will nearly always be better than air straight from the street. Many city councils have realized that street pollution is one of the chief causes of ill health and are implementing measures to reduce traffic and the resulting pollution in residential areas.

Gas, coal and wood-burning fireplaces and stoves are all

< up the garden path
If you live in a built-up residential area, use a coir doormat or have a front path made from wood chippings, sand or sea shells to clean the grime from your shoes before you enter your home.

potential sources of air pollution, especially if they produce smoke or if you allow the gases to come into your home. If they are sealed, have controlled air inlets and flues leading outdoors, and are properly maintained, they should not be a problem. Although smoky fuels are generally very bad for your health, smokeless fuels can be even more harmful because you can't see the pollution they produce. Poorly maintained gas fireplaces with bad ventilation, and air-starved heaters, create carbon monoxide, which can kill silently while you're asleep. If your kitchen has a gas stove, make sure you have a good extract ventilation system to prevent the buildup of dangerous combustion gases, such as carbon monoxide and nitrogen dioxide, and buy a carbon monoxide detector to be sure your home is safe.

Radon

In some parts of the world, pollution also seeps up from the ground in the form of radon, a naturally occurring radioactive gas. Radon rises from underground rocks and flows into homes through poorly sealed floors. Local authorities will be able to tell you whether radon is a problem in your area and will also advise on how to reduce its hazards. The basic method for reducing radon is to seal the ground floor and draw underground gases away from your home by extracting air either from an underground well or from the void under a raised wood ground floor. Good ventilation in the home will also help to reduce radon; you might even consider installing a heat recovery ventilation system that provides a constant but low-energy air cleaning system (see page 40).

Natural air fresheners

Rather than use mass-produced air fresheners, keep your home clean and fresh by choosing nontoxic furniture and floor finishes, preventing moisture buildup in bathrooms and kitchens, and implementing a no-smoking policy. If you want to scent the air, use fresh flowers, herbs and essential oils. Suitable flowers that add a pleasant aroma to your surroundings include fresh-cut honeysuckle, jasmine and roses. Crush fresh lavender, thyme and lemon balm and keep them in bowls in different parts of the home to benefit from their scent. Burning essential oils such as

< **kitchen freshness**
An extractor fan above the stove will absorb cooking smells and remove excess heat, preventing these from spreading to other parts of your home.

sandalwood and amber or adding them to soaps will also help to cover up any unpleasant cooking odors in your home.

Ionizers

Thought by some people to keep the air cleaner, ionizers come in two types. The simpler one draws in air and gives particles of dust a negative charge. Walls and floors in the room become relatively positively charged and dirt is then attracted to the nearest surface. This results in cleaner air but dirtier walls. However, you will at least be able to see the dirt in order to clean it away. The negatively charged air also counteracts the positive charges that come off electrical equipment.

The second type is an electrostatic filter that ionizes the air but also contains a positively charged filter element that catches dust as it passes through the machine. The air that returns to the room should consequently be neutral and clean.

There is little scientific evidence that ionizers will really improve your life, but many people swear by them. If you've tried everything else and failed, then borrow an ionizer from a friend or ask to test-drive one before purchasing.

VENTILATION

Many specialists feel that modern homes are underventilated and consequently prone to internal

pollution. In fact, very few homes are completely airtight and many leak like a sieve. This is true of old and new buildings alike, and some older buildings often feel like they are more air than wall! The only truly airtight buildings are specially built by architects who use high-quality techniques to seal every gap in the outside wall. Since these are rare, you should assume that if your home is stuffy or makes you ill, the problem is more likely to do with the materials and appliances in your home (see chapter 3) or the way your home is mechanically ventilated.

Rooms that do require additional ventilation are bathrooms, toilets and kitchens. In essence, you should have a mechanical ventilation system to remove smells, control dampness and pollution, and ensure that heat is not wasted by opening windows in cold weather. Heat recovery ventilation systems can also be used to improve the quality of ventilation in your home.

< household helpers
One of the best-known indoor air cleaners is the spider plant, whose leaves absorb formaldehyde from carpets. Chrysanthemums and azaleas are also known to remove chemicals from the air during photosynthesis, while perfuming your home in the process.

Other ventilation options are passive vents that are found in the attics of many homes. These let air into a room without the need to open any windows. They can be fitted with small sliders so you can adjust the level of ventilation to suit the changing climate and your personal requirements.

Dampness

Poor ventilation is just one of the causes of damp air and surfaces, a problem that can make our homes smell, encourage microbes and cause asthma and bronchial illnesses. To solve moisture problems, find the cause rather than treating the effect. Dampness in modern buildings is caused by hidden leaks and poor building work, as well as poor ventilation. In older buildings, dampness can also occur if water penetrates solid walls or rises through unsealed ground floors. If you can't find the cause of your problem, seek the advice of an independent home inspector. Dampness from faulty plumbing or leaking drains, flashing and tiles can be resolved by fixing the problem at its source. As for damaged or missing waterproof membranes (plastic or rubber sheets that stop buildings from getting wet), these should be replaced and all surfaces will need to be treated with moisture-repellent paints. Unfortunately, some waterproofing techniques may create pollution themselves. The worst culprits are chemical injection kits that stop moisture from rising in external brickwork. Far better than these, although more expensive, is to install a new waterproof course in the faulty area using traditional materials such as slate.

∨ an airy room

Well-designed windows provide controlled access to daylight and clean, fresh air. Open them in summer for a cool breeze, but use passive vents in the winter to prevent heat loss. Ventilation is vitally important if you have a hobby involving potentially toxic materials, such as glues or paints. Better still, choose eco-friendly paints.

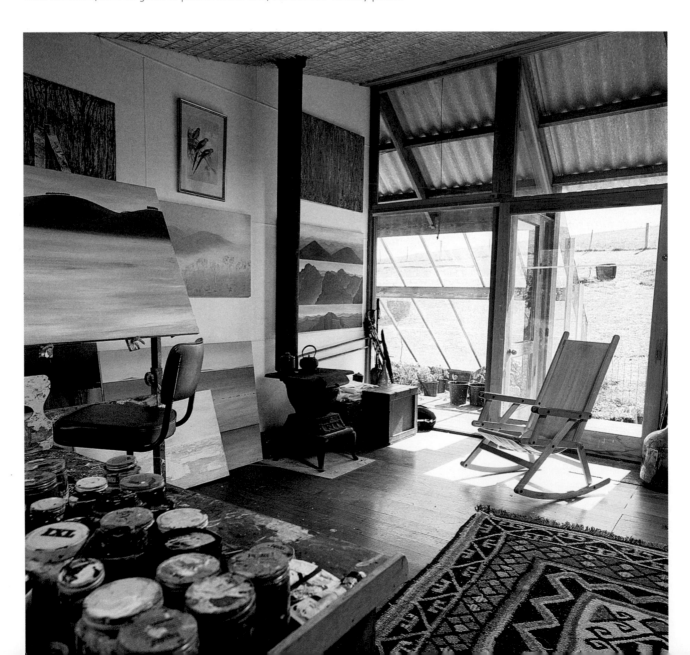

Conserving water

Water, like air, is vital to our lives. Yet so often it is demoted to a dull necessity, left to be dealt with by plumbers and forgotten during decorating. Water is, in fact, one of the most calming and cleansing elements available, both aesthetically and ecologically.

Rather than relying totally on the complex system of reservoirs, chemical treatment, pumping stations, pipework and sewers created by utility companies, we can put some of our faith in the natural cycle of water. This involves collecting rainwater from our roofs, storing it safely in cool underground tanks and using it for many of our water needs. Using sensible conservation techniques, we can reduce our demand for water by at least 50 percent. At the same time we can create an exciting addition to our homes.

HARVESTING RAINWATER

The roof of a typical European home can collect enough water to supply a family of three with most of its annual water needs.

The first stage of reusing rainwater is to simply store it in a couple of plastic barrels for use in the garden or for washing outdoor equipment. The next stage is to construct a plastic or concrete tank underground where the water will remain cool and clean. The low temperature is an important aspect because dangerous bacteria does not grow in cool water.

collecting water
Water can be collected and recycled on a small scale (above), or a larger-scale tank (right) can be used to collect water for most of a household's needs.

While rainwater is basically safe, many areas of the world (cities especially) have high levels of air pollution, making the direct use of rainwater for drinking potentially harmful (although it can be filtered). Rainwater quality is much better in rural areas, but you still need to ensure that the roof collecting it is lead free. Make sure that all lead flashings have been removed and that the roof is not made from zinc or asbestos.

DRINKING WATER

We drink only 3 percent of the water delivered to our homes, yet it is all purified and chemically treated at vast expense, sometimes even to dubious quality. This water is often treated with chlorine and

< **dishwashing by hand**
If you generate only a small amount of dirty dishes, it is more ecological and economical to wash dishes by hand.

ECO-TIP

Water safety

Even in the developed world, water-borne diseases remain a constant threat. To prevent this, inspect your water tank regularly, watching for water stagnation. Also, make sure that all your pipework and fittings are clean and free of growth. If cold water is stored below 60°F and hot water above 130°F, then any bacteria will either die or lie dormant. If water is between these temperatures, you are at risk from Legionnaires' disease (a form of pneumonia), especially if you are old or unwell.

---

fluoride, which is good for teeth, but some people find the taste unpleasant. Buying bottles of imported mineral water is not an ecological solution, because the process used to manufacture and transport it is far less efficient than that for treating tap or rainwater. Simple pitcher-based carbon filters are a cheap and relatively effective way to improve the taste of drinking water, but make sure you change the filter frequently. You can also buy more expensive whole-house or tap-based filter systems that provide a one-stop solution for removing hardness from water while also ensuring it is chemically clean.

HOUSEHOLD APPLIANCES

One of the great successes of environmental awareness has been the development of household appliances that combine time-saving effectiveness with ecological respect. While some manufacturers have always considered water and energy

conservation an important part of the design, the majority have felt that price and look were the only selling points. Now that Europe, Scandinavia and the United States have developed eco-labeling and Energy Star certification, we can see clearly how one product compares with the others. If we all choose A-rated appliances and use them wisely, we will not only save money in the short term, but we will also help to reduce the effects of pollution and water shortage on our planet in the future.

Dishwashers

While older dishwashing machines used large quantities of water, A-rated dishwashers actually use less water and energy than washing by hand. This is because they sense the dirtiness of the water and decide whether it can be used twice. They also use hot water from one cycle to warm the water in the next, and use cold water to condense steam so the dishes can be dried with air alone. These new dishwashers can clean a whole day's dirty dishes with less than 3 gallons of water (see page 166). Dishwashers require detergents that are harsher than hand-dishwashing liquid, but eco-friendly alternatives are available.

Washing machines

Albeit great labor-saving devices, washing machines have only recently become water and energy efficient. Like dishwashers, A-rated washing machines monitor the dirtiness of rinse water, recycle hot water, and have numerous settings appropriate for different loads. They still consume more than 13 gallons of water for each wash, so it is best to save your dirty laundry until you have a full load and dry your clothes on the line rather than tumbling them in a restricted drier; they'll smell fresher, have fewer creases and save energy.

WATER PIPES

In the past, before its toxicity was common knowledge, lead was used in some water pipes. If your house is more than forty years old, check with a plumber to make sure your pipes are safe, because water running over lead can cause this metal to accumulate in the body, resulting in mental retardation, hypertension and impaired immune response. The most eco-friendly piping available today is polypropylene plastic for hot water pipes and polyethylene for cold water systems. These materials do not corrode and their production uses less energy than that of steel or copper pipes. Stainless-steel pipes may be preferable for exposed locations since they are attractive and are easy to recycle at the end of their lives. Copper

LIVING NATURALLY

Conserving water

The average household uses about 42 gallons of water per day, nearly all of which is treated, pumped, then dumped. The following are some simple practices that can reduce this figure:

• Never let tap water run when drinking it. Use a glass instead.

• Use a plug in kitchen sinks and bathroom basins.

• Fix leaking taps immediately and consider installing aerating taps that halve water flow.

• Run a bath only when you have the time to luxuriate in it and share it with someone!

• Don't use kitchen waste disposal units because these waste water and also eliminate valuable compost.

• Take quick showers instead of a bath.

• Install a dual-flush toilet, which gives you the option of flushing with a small or a large dose of water. Alternatively, put a brick in the tank. A more radical option is to install a zero water toilet.

• Collect and filter rainwater (see page 33) to use in baths, showers, washing machines and gardens.

pipes are still commonly used, but they do cause some water pollution that is harmful to water-borne organisms.

All hot water pipes should be insulated to keep water warm, and the distance between the hot water source and taps should be as short as possible. If you live in a cold climate, you should also insulate cold water pipes and tanks in attics and basements to prevent them from freezing and bursting.

Ceramic remains the best material for drains since it creates less pollution than plastic alternatives during production. If you use plastic drains, avoid PVC because this is more toxic and harder to dispose of than polypropylene.

RESTORATIVE QUALITIES

In Eastern philosophies, water is a very important element. It is also a key factor in design, both in the home and in the garden. In winter, leave wide bowls of water with incense or floating candles to create a relaxing atmosphere in a room and add moisture to dry air. In summer, follow an old Indian custom and fill leaky clay pots with water, then wrap them in muslin cloth and leave by an open window. The breeze will help the water to evaporate, thus chilling the air.

In the garden, water supports a diverse range of flora and fauna, from reeds and lilies to frogs and water boatmen. These come into their own during summer, when the garden pool becomes a thriving living community.

If you have a large garden, clean and reuse waste water from sinks and baths by installing a gray-water filtering system. If you are going to do this, don't use dangerous chemicals, such as chlorine and ammonia, in your house (see page 165 for alternatives). Drain gray water (the term for water from sinks and

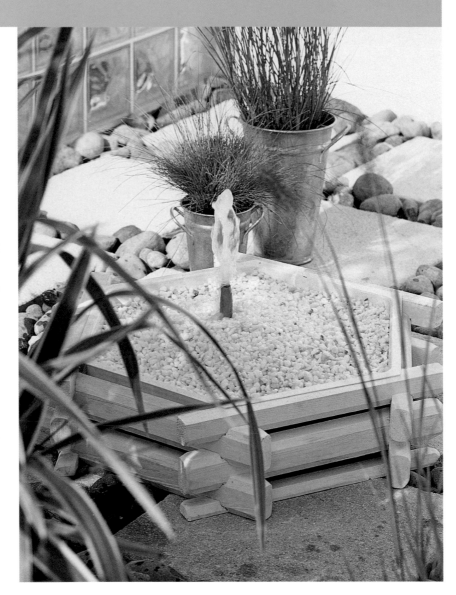

∧ soothing water
The sound of trickling water makes your garden a calming and supportive place in which to spend time. Rather than feeding an outdoor water feature or pond with chlorinated tap water, maintain it with rainwater from your roof or divert water from hard paving in the garden.

baths) from your home into a gravel bed where reeds and other water-loving plants are grown. Bacteria that feed on nutrients in the water will help to break down the more complex chemicals, and

water from the reed bed will eventually drain through the gravel to a second bed, then into a pond that can feed other garden plants or else flow safely away into streams.

Heating
your home

In the temperate world, half of all the energy consumed in the home is used for heating, yet with careful design it is quite possible to halve this figure. In cities, the best heating systems to have are gas-fueled ones, while wood-fueled heaters are good for country homes. Never use electricity for heating because it creates three times as much pollution as a high-efficiency gas heater. Other inefficient heating sources include older gas fireplaces and heaters. Open wood-burning fireplaces are also inefficient, not to mention polluting, so avoid these as well. The best eco-option is to have solar panels, which will preheat water, but your home needs to have a south-facing garden or roof. They are quite expensive, so make sure you consider the simpler and cheaper options first.

INSULATION

Just like a warm coat, a cozy home needs to be well insulated,

> a warm glow

Fireplaces provide a focal point in many homes but should be used sparingly since they are inefficient and create pollution. In mild weather, though, lighting a fire in the sitting room may be more efficient than turning on the central heating.

with tight-fitting openings. The cost of insulating your home depends on the way it was originally built. Simple techniques, such as roof insulation, may pay back in one or two years, while major renovations, such as double glazing, may take ten years to recoup the original outlay. The benefits in comfort, energy saving and ecological responsibility are well worth considering, however.

Roofs

This is the easiest part of the home to insulate, particularly if you have an attic. Cellulose insulation is made from recycled paper and 6 to 8 inches of it will reduce to almost zero the heat lost through your roof. The paper is pretreated with environmentally sensitive fire and animal repellent and is blown into the roof void via an air blower (basically a vacuum cleaner in reverse). The paper lies in the space, keeping heat in and reducing noise from rain.

Other eco-insulation materials include sheep's wool (marketed as Climawool) and corkboard. Less benign materials include glass and mineral fiber mats, various expanded plastics and loose-fill heat-blown vermiculite.

When insulating roofs, remember to keep eave vents clear so that moisture doesn't build up and cause damage from condensation. You should also carry out all carpentry, plumbing and electrical work before laying down insulation. Finally, make sure you protect insulation from hot flues, recessed lighting and electrical wiring to avoid heat damage.

DEGREES OF ENERGY SAVING

When it comes to energy saving, it's best to start with simple measures that have a large impact, then move toward more complex and expensive tasks.

Simple changes

Install weather stripping around window and door frames.
Install heavy curtains to windows and close them at night.
Place door stoppers by doors.
Fill gaps under skirting boards with newspaper or sealant.
Install additional insulation in the attic or crawl space.
Insulate the water heater and hot water pipes.
Install a timer and thermostat for your heating system.

Medium-effort changes

Install thermostatic radiator valves on room radiators.
Add storm doors to front and back doors.
Add solar stores (see page 42) to catch the heat in sun-facing rooms.

Changes requiring significant effort and money

Replace old furnaces or electric heating systems with modern high-efficiency condensing gas heaters.
Replace old and leaky windows with new double-glazed units or install secondary windows behind traditional hard-to-replace windows in older homes.
Add solar conservatories to sun-facing rooms and buffer spaces to north-facing ones.

More expensive solutions

Fit solar panels on the roof and south-facing walls.
Add additional insulation to walls and floors.
Install a home heat-recovery ventilation system to replace individual extract fans in kitchens and bathrooms.

Floors

The simplest way of insulating ground floors is to install insulation under the final floor covering. From an ecological perspective, the greenest material is corkboard because it is a naturally renewable material. It is also water and vermin resistant and easy to lay. The cheapest material for floor insulation is probably expanded polystyrene board. This provides good insulation and is also easy to lay, but its environmental credentials are not as good as those of cork.

If you have a raised timber ground floor then you can achieve very good insulation by installing cellulose fiber between the floor joists. This is simply lain on top of a breather layer or fiberboard that is supported from the joists. Make sure that you do not block air vents, since this will cause dampness and consequent damage.

Windows

Area for area, windows are the leakiest part of your home. A single sheet of glass provides hardly any insulation at all. Double glazing, by contrast, traps a layer of insulating air between the two panes of glass, halving the amount of heat loss compared with single-glazed windows. Even more energy-conserving types of window are now available. One of these is known as low-e (emissivity) glazing. This consists

∧ **keeping the heat in**

Thick and lined floor-to-ceiling curtains keep heat in and drafts out, while adding color and texture to your home. If you have radiators beneath your windows, it is a good idea to move them to an internal wall, otherwise much of the heat they produce will escape outside.

walls are cavity walls that comprise two brick or concrete blocks with a void in between. These can be insulated (if they aren't already) by injecting mineral fiber into the void. While not an environmentally benign process, the resulting reduction in your heat and energy expenditure makes it a good long-term option.

Older homes built with solid walls can be insulated by installing an internal or external lining of insulation. Internal insulation involves building a wall of furring strips on the inside of the external walls that need insulation. Cellulose fiber or mineral fiber panels fill the cavity between the furring strips, and the wall is then covered in a final layer of plasterboard. The

of a thin layer of transparent plastic film between the panes of glass, which bounces heat back into the room. Another option is to choose glazed windows with argon gas (a better insulator than air) between the panes. The really eco-conscious may prefer triple-glazed windows with argon gas and low-e film; these let more heat into your home than they lose, which, in effect, make them heaters without the ongoing expense!

If you are in the enviable position of building your own home, it will be more energy efficient to install more windows on sun-facing elevations and fewer on north-facing ones (and obviously the reverse if you live in the southern hemisphere). Remember, however, to provide some shading on south- or west-facing windows, to prevent your home from overheating in summer.

Walls

Insulating walls is more complex but can be just as important, particularly if your home is in a cold, windy and exposed location. Most modern external

∧ **warm walls**

A fully renewable natural material, wool makes an excellent insulant. It is highly efficient at trapping air and therefore heat, absorbing moisture from the air and providing sound insulation.

downside of internal insulation is that rooms become slightly smaller, but a small warm room is far better than a large cold one!

External insulation is often applied to homes that are badly affected by moisture. This involves fixing mineral fiber slabs to the outside walls, then rendering the surface with plaster to create a water and damage-resistant finish that you can paint.

EFFICIENT HEATING

If your home is small and well-insulated, it is best to concentrate all your heating in one room and let adjacent rooms warm up by heat's natural movement through walls and air. One way of achieving this is by installing a small gas or wood-fired stove in the living room, which is where you spend most of your time. Wood stoves (see below right) with secondary combustion chambers will halve the amount of logs

heat recovery ventilation systems

These suck warm stale air out of rooms, absorbing the heat from the air into a metal heat exchanger and transferring the warmth into fresh air, which is then blown into living rooms or circulation spaces. Homes with these systems have lower heating bills and are free from drafts, provided that windows are properly sealed and passive air vents closed. The one downside is that the running fans can consume more energy than is saved by recovering heat. To avoid this, buy units with small variable speed fans sized for your needs and use humidity-controlled grilles that turn the unit off when air is dry.

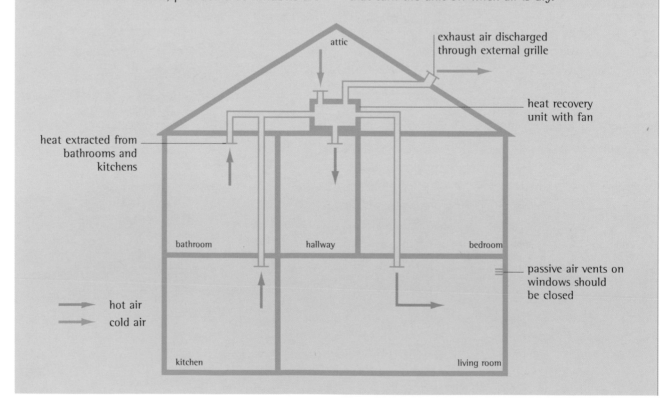

attic

exhaust air discharged through external grille

heat recovery unit with fan

heat extracted from bathrooms and kitchens

bathroom   hallway   bedroom

passive air vents on windows should be closed

→ hot air
→ cold air

kitchen   living room

required and reduce emissions through the chimney.

In larger homes, it is probably best to install a central heating system with a single boiler and radiators in each room. A good central heating system uses a condensing boiler, so-called because even the heat in the exhaust gas is condensed out of them. Condensing boilers are 90 percent efficient, saving you significant sums of money and energy over their lifetime. If you are installing the system from scratch, design it to run at a low temperature (105–125°F rather than the traditional 160–180°F), since this ensures the boiler is running at high efficiency all the time.

To control when the boiler operates, use a timer and easily adjustable thermostat. You can also install thermostatic radiator

valves, which allow you to set the temperature in each room. Boiler manufacturers have developed complex controls; the more you spend, the more functions you have and these programmable controllers are definitely cost-effective in larger homes.

A low-energy alternative to radiators is under-floor heating. Plastic heating pipes are fitted into the floor, either in a cement screed or in chipboard panels. Because they warm the floor rather than the air, homes with under-floor heating can be kept a couple of degrees cooler, which will save you up to 20 percent on your heating bill.

Efficient hot water

Generally, water is heated by a water heater, which is fueled by either gas or electricity. These systems tend to lose lots of heat through the miles of copper tubing employed in their design. Keep the water heater and pipes well insulated, set the thermostat at 130°F and use a time switch that turns the heater on only when you need hot water.

In new homes, you may find that mains pressure combination

< cozy warmth
Wood burning stoves not only heat the room they occupy, they can also generate enough energy to warm water.

> ### ECO-TIP
>
> **Shelter belts**
> Plants and animals instinctively find places that provide them with maximum protection from winter winds, and we too can use nature to shelter our homes. Planting trees and hedges around our homes or growing evergreen climbers over wind-facing walls will halve the speed of the wind. Not only does this make our homes warmer, it also protects our gardens from the stress of high winds and driving rain. The most successful shelter belts combine both deciduous and evergreen planting: evergreen trees and bushes grown at a distance from your house will protect it from wind, while deciduous trees will allow the sun to warm your home in winter.

condensing boilers provide a more efficient source of warm water. Commonly known as combi boilers, these only fire up when there is a demand for warm water, although good ones will have a miniature storage tank so you don't have to wait for hot water to appear at the tap.

SOLAR HEATING

While winter is often cold and dark, there are still many days when the sun comes out. On these days, sun-facing rooms in your home can collect heat and solar stores can trap the heat for later in the day. Solar stores are dark, heavy surfaces inside the home that warm up when hit by the sun. At night they keep rooms warmer without the need for additional heating. Heavyweight homes that have concrete floors and brick walls are natural solar stores. Lightweight homes of wood and plasterboard require a little more ingenuity. Some architects place barrels of water inside rooms, since these have a huge thermal mass that absorbs heat well. If the floor can take the weight, another option is to lay slates or tile walls in sunny parts of your home.

∧ the old and the new

You don't need to live in an ultramodern home to consider solar-powered heating. In fact, the only requirement is that you have a south-facing roof that gets plenty of sunshine. Sometimes the clean design of solar panels can actually complement more traditional architectural styles.

Solar-powered hot water

If your home has a south-facing roof or sunny garden, installing solar panels can halve your hot water bill and provide you with free hot water throughout the summer. Some heat can even be collected on cloudy days, but you'll still need a water heater for dark winter days.

Solar panels are usually installed on your roof, where they collect the sun's energy and transfer the heat to your home's hot water storage tank. They are best located above any overshadowing trees or buildings and should face between southeast and southwest. Obviously, the amount of sunshine varies depending where you live, and this will affect the type of solar panel you need. There is a huge range of options, each with its own pros and cons. Evacuated tube systems are more expensive but are also more efficient, while flat plate systems are cheaper but larger. You can even make your own by painting radiators black and putting them in a poly tunnel in the garden.

The amount of money you save will depend on the type of heating system you have. If you have a gas water heater, it will take twenty to thirty years to make back the money invested in solar panels, but knowing you are doing your bit for the environment will make the investment worthwhile.

Keeping cool

In warm climates, the number of homes with air-conditioning is growing at an alarming rate. While this modern convenience gives a perceived improvement in comfort over the short term, it creates a highly artificial environment and brings with it many health risks. It is much better to instead make use of natural passive cooling.

The ideal way to protect your home from overheating is to use plants as shade providers, breeze collectors and climate modifiers. A

keep your cool
Wooden shutters (above) keep sunshine out while allowing breezes to circulate. An arbor (right) offers some welcome shade.

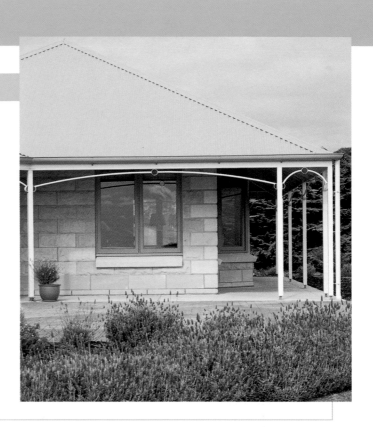

LIVING NATURALLY

Protection from the sun

If your home is overheating because of a poorly designed roof, consider the following:

• Installing heat-reflecting aluminum foil and insulation in the attic space or under the roof tiles to reduce heat buildup in the roof.

• Increasing ventilation to the attic space by adding some wall vents and wind chimneys that catch the prevailing breeze.

• Building your roof out over sun-facing east and west sides of your home to protect it from direct sunlight.

• Painting metal roofs a light color to reflect heat. Special paints that reflect more than two-thirds of the sun's heat are now available in most hardware stores.

good planting design can reduce the temperature of the ground around your home by up to 20°F. Deciduous trees to the west and south will protect your home from the summer sun but allow winter sun through. While plants won't prevent the heat from high-level midday sun, they will provide shade in the early morning and late afternoon. Tree and vine belts to the east and west of your home give the best protection. Vines and thick-leafed plants can also shade windows and walls from sun that is reflected off the ground.

SHADING YOUR HOME

By attaching external awnings to your windows, you not only keep solar heat out of the house, you also protect paint from peeling. Indoor blinds, slatted shutters and overhanging roofs use the same principle to keep you cool.

Arbors are perhaps the simplest way of shading your home while

providing additional living space on dry days. These are best built from wood posts and beams that can support layers of shade cloth. They can also provide surfaces for vines and climbers to grow along.

Once you have protected your home from the sun, you need to make the best use of the cool night air and prevailing winds to make your home comfortable on the hottest days. The windows and internal doors of your home should be designed so that breezes can flow through your house day

< cool cooking
An external awning and ceiling fan will help to keep the kitchen—usually the hottest room in the house—cool.

and night. You also need to consider associated issues, such as security, acoustics and protection from weather. If your windows have external slatted shutters, they should be burglar proof, with the windows opening inward. Also, make sure external awnings and verandas are designed to withstand strong winds and heavy rain. To make the most of night ventilation, your home should be constructed of heavy materials that will absorb the cool of the night and so keep your home cooler in the day.

KEEPING COOL INDOORS

In hot and dry climates, reduce the temperature in your home by using evaporative water cooling. You can do this either by placing muslin-wrapped clay jugs of water on window sills or by using an evaporative cooler, which cools the air by spraying water into a fan-assisted air stream.

If all else fails, consider using air-conditioning for some of the time. Traditional through-the-wall units are inexpensive but inefficient solutions. Instead, buy air-conditioners with high-efficiency compressors because these reduce electrical demand to a minimum. Also, only turn them on when it's absolutely necessary.

MADE IN GREECE

Cool interiors

In hot Mediterranean countries, houses are often designed with thick walls, small windows, internal courtyards and white rendered walls because these features provide comfortable living conditions without the need for expensive, energy-consuming air-conditioning. Commonly found in Greece and Spain, these homes often have cooler interiors than modern air-conditioned hotels.

Color, texture and pattern

Aquick and easy way to stamp your unique personality on a space is to treat it to a few licks of paint and some interesting fabric throws.

CHOOSING COLORS

To decide on a color scheme, you need to understand how color affects space and your moods. Because dark surfaces absorb light while light surfaces reflect it, dark colors make a room feel smaller, while light colors make a room seem larger. In the same way, dark colors absorb heat, so painting a sunny room in darker colors will make it warmer than painting it with a pale, light color will.

The ideal color scheme for an eco-home therefore varies depending upon the weather and the time of year. On dark days, light surfaces will help to brighten your home while on sunny winter days darker furnishings can be used in south-facing rooms to capture some of the sun's warmth.

Natural colors

Nowadays you can get dyes in any color under the sun, chiefly due to the amazing technical advances made in the chemical industry. The synthetic dye industry uses many heavy metal salts and oxides to make everything from brilliant

creative illusions

A large space will feel intimate and cozy if it is decorated with solid materials and dark colors (left). Similarly, a small space will have a light and airy atmosphere if it is decorated with pale colors (above).

white (titanium) to acid yellow (chrome). Yet, many of these metals are toxic and can pollute our water supply. Instead, we should opt for fabrics colored by natural dyes, which are not only beautiful, but also harmless.

Earth pigments are based on colors found in natural earth sources and vary in color from traditional browns, such as burnt sienna and red ochre, to deep grays and blacks. Mineral

pigments are created using similar techniques to those used in the mainstream chemical industry but rely on known-to-be-safe minerals. These dyes are supplied as powder pigments that are mixed into neutral paints to create a huge variety of colors and shades. For more information on choosing paints and dyes see page 66.

< color swatches

Before you go ahead and choose a color scheme, use swatches in various shades to get a more complete feel for each of their effects.

unless you are absolutely sure that they will work, perhaps because you have seen them in a friend's home.

A single wall of strong color against a neutral background often works more successfully than a room immersed entirely in strong color. Similarly, a common color theme throughout your home will be more successful than a series of contrasting colors.

Neutral colors will frame and compose furniture, decorations and flowers more successfully than strong color schemes, but bright color schemes do work well with neutral furniture and decorations.

PATTERNS AND TEXTURES

Like color, different patterns and textures can influence the atmosphere, perceived space and mood of your home. If your rooms don't feel quite large enough, you could consider using patterned

Creating mood with color

Although color is a very personal experience, there are some general rules to follow when deciding on color schemes for different parts of your home.

Bedrooms are restful, calming places that need to work both on dark winter mornings and on bright summer days. You should therefore decorate these rooms with light shades, since they will encourage you to wake up. Avoid colors that are too cool, such as bright blues, or warm reds and oranges, since these are either too stimulating or too soporific.

Living rooms can afford to be painted in brighter colors, although neutral color schemes will work equally well. Avoid strong colors over large areas

> simple solutions

Incorporating texture and patterns into your home doesn't have to be an expensive or arduous job. Simple and natural elements can be used to great effect and minimal cost.

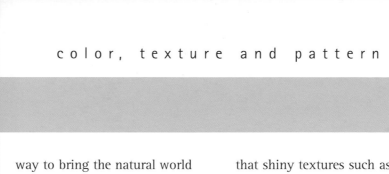

wallpapers and fabrics to create the illusion of space. Horizontal stripes help to widen a space, while vertical stripes can give the illusion of height to a room. Use these techniques carefully, since the resulting pattern can over-whelm everything else. Although pattern used en masse can be overwhelming, a wall of repeated form can create a stimulating backdrop in a neutral room.

Natural patterns
Throughout the ages, these have inspired all kinds of artworks. You can bring these patterns into your home directly by exposing the grain of wood in furniture and other objects, or by displaying the subtle and varied colors of polished or raw stones and slates. Handmade fabrics colored with plant dyes capture the accidental flaws of natural materials. And print and computer processes allow modern designers to uncover new natural patterns, with the fractal world of atomic particles and organic growth patterns found in leaves, shells and items of nature.

Texture
Texture is about touch and shape as well as pattern, and it is a great way to bring the natural world into your home. A textural home is, in essence, a visual and tactile massage, with the rough scratch of fiber rugs or the calm and cool surface of a sea-worn beach pebble. Introducing the flotsam and jetsam of the natural world into your home can make the plainest of corners a fond memory and a visual delight.

The texture of an item will affect how easy it is on the eye. Use soft-textured, light-absorbing materials such as fabrics to balance the harsher effects of reflective surfaces. And remember that shiny textures such as gloss paint or ceramic tiles will stand out more than velvety or rough textures such as brick.

v paint effects
You can add depth and warmth to your color scheme by using special techniques for applying paint. Different brushes and combs will allow you to achieve a whole variety of effects, such as the "denim" look of this bedroom wall.

3 Eco-materials

Materials matter. They provide us with a framework around which
we build our homes and are the surfaces that we see, feel and walk
on. Just as important, they have an impact on the world around us,
improving or scarring the land; providing prosperity or poverty,
health or illness; and creating beauty or ugliness. Your choice of
materials should therefore be based on more than just price,
convenience and fashion. Instead, consider how you can make your
home connect with the world around you, capturing the beauty of
the natural world and stimulating your senses and your mind.

What makes an eco-material?

Eco-materials must reflect your own way of living and your particular take on the world. Without this, they will quickly bore you and be changed for something new (this throw-away culture is not particularly eco-friendly). For some, the fundamental choice of how to decorate and fill the home may be to create a place of softness and ease; for others, one of sparseness that provides room to think clearly and change rapidly.

There are a number of factors that define eco-materials. They grow naturally or are plentiful; need little energy to make, deliver and care for; are nontoxic and easy to clean; are long lasting; provide both local and global communities with decent livelihoods; and are easy to reuse when they come to the end of their lives. Often, they may be passed down by older generations from a time when beauty, durability and craftsmanship were the only recognized ways of making things.

Similarly, good designs are healthy and ergonomic, lasting well beyond the dictates of fashion, and aging with you. They are also safe for children and the less able. They might be made from recycled materials, but they should always be practical, fun and tasteful.

> hand me down
Always try to buy classic, good-quality furniture made from long-lasting materials such as wood, metal or leather. These will serve you well throughout their lifetime in your home but will also be appreciated down the family line for generations to come.

The guide on pages 174–83 provides an eco-rating for many of the materials you are likely to find around your home, and this chapter guides you through the range of materials you can choose to decorate and furnish your home. From the surfaces you stand on and lean against to the furniture you lounge on, the utensils you cook with, the fabrics you drape, the clothes you wear, and even the garden path you stroll along, you will discover what sort of materials are best

< suitable materials
Generally speaking, materials can be divided into four categories: those that grow naturally, such as wood, grasses and animal skins (top); those that are rare resources, such as metal and oil (far left); those that are plentiful and safe, such as stone, gravel and sand (immediate left); and those that are toxic, such as lead or solvents. All but the toxic have a place in our homes.

Learning about the energy needed to make finishes and furniture is one way to discover the environmental impact of goods we buy. The chart below shows the energy measured in gigajoules (GJ) needed to produce a metric ton of some common building materials.

Material	Energy (GJ)
Very high energy	
Aluminum	200–250
Plastics	50–100
Copper	100+
Stainless steel	100+
High energy	
Steel	30–60
Lead, zinc	25+
Glass	12–25
Plasterboard	8–10
Medium energy	
Lime	3–5
Clay bricks and tiles	2–7
Gypsum plaster	1–4
Concrete:	
in situ	0.8–1.5
blocks	0.8–3.5
precast	1.5–8
Sand lime bricks	0.8–1.2
Wood	0.1–5
Low energy	
Sand, aggregate	< 0.5
Fly ash, RHA,	
volcanic ash	< 0.5
Soil	< 0.5

suited to which parts of your home, for your own and your family's health, for ease of maintenance and, of course, for the benefit of the planet.

Your personal circumstances will also affect the choices you make about the materials for your home. Ask yourself how long you intend to stay where you live and how your life will change while you are there. What influences do your partner, your children or your work life have on how you live at home? If you are often on the move, choose small and portable furnishings that you can take with you. And if you have children, favor hard-wearing and easy-to-clean items.

Finally, no matter what the advertisers or eco-activists say, natural does not always mean good and synthetic doesn't always mean bad. It may, in fact, be better to build a house from recycled steel than from poorly managed forest timber and reuse eco-friendly plastic bags instead of recycled paper ones.

Floor
foundations

The floor has to withstand the brunt of our fast, heavy and messy lifestyle. Yet good flooring really does act as a physical and decorative key, connecting rooms together and, when carefully chosen, helping us to maintain our homes as clean and healthy places.

THE SUBFLOOR

Underneath your floor is, for want of a better word, the subfloor. This flat surface supports the weight of you and your furniture and takes your choice of floor finish. In most homes, the subfloor will be made from either wood or concrete. These materials have different characteristics that can be exploited to your advantage. Before considering any further floor covering, however, check to make sure that the existing subfloor is sound (see chart opposite).

Concrete subfloors

These are generally found in modern buildings or in the basements of older homes and can be sealed, painted and waxed to provide easy-to-clean floor finishes in their own right. Most available concrete sealants are derived from petrochemicals and are not particularly eco-friendly, although the sheer simplicity of the sealant means that very little

> **for warm climates**
> A polished concrete finish not only obviates the need for further floor coverings but also looks stylish and feels cool underfoot.

energy or material is wasted in its production. Concrete floors that are polished brick red are reminiscent of waxed earth floors found throughout Africa, while white painted concrete floors create a bright and thoroughly modern floor finish that can brighten darker rooms. To create a softer effect, lay down rugs.

The benefits of concrete subfloors include the fact that they help homes in temperate climates to remain comfortable on cold days because they absorb heat, spreading warmth into the night. They also provide sound insulation between floors and are easy to keep clean, provided that they are sealed. They require little more than a good sweep and the occasional mop, which makes them ideal for kitchens.

The downside is that they are not particularly comfortable to walk on and can make your home a noisy place, particularly if you have kids running around. They can be a source of moisture in older homes and basements and may need to be

sealed with waterproof rendering. They can also be treacherous when wet, even if painted with slip-resistant sealant.

Wooden subfloors

Wood joists form the basis for subfloors in most older homes and often in many new ones. The space between floor joists is commonly used to route water pipes and electrical cables, so consider future access needs before laying any further flooring on top. Wood floorboards are best sealed with eco-friendly natural waxes and oils to resist damage from water and other substances. Natural wood stains come in a variety of colors, from white spruce through to ebony, and also in a wide range of both opaque and translucent colors.

The benefit of wood subfloors is their ability to last for many years if properly cared for, remaining strong and resilient while aging gracefully. Repairing existing softwood floorboards can also be a relatively cheap way to improve your home. You can do this by taking up old wall-to-wall carpeting, removing any nails, mending creaking planks, then sanding and polishing with natural wax and oils.

The downside is that noise can easily travel through wood floors. However, this can be rectified by placing insulation material between the joists (the best eco-insulation is made from recycled paper that has been treated against fires and insects). Ideally the final floor finish should be separated from the joists by an insulating mat to create a floating floor.

Another potential problem is that wood joists might not be able to take the weight of additional heavy floor covering. If you have doubts, ask your flooring supplier to check the structural capacity of your existing floor.

Finally, wood floors will not last well in wet environments, so avoid them in bathrooms. They can be used in kitchens provided you are careful to clean up water spills immediately.

While many environmental designers prefer the lightweight solution offered by wood floors, a concrete slab does not use a great deal of energy but provides thermal mass, which helps to keep your home warm in winter and cool in summer. Either way, insulate the ground floor by using expanded polystyrene under concrete floors and cellulose or mineral fiber insulation between the joists in wood floors (see page 38).

Upper floors, however, are best made from wood joists because they are light and easy to install or modify. Concrete is heavy, requiring additional steel reinforcement, stronger supporting walls and deeper foundations when used for upper floors, and is almost impossible to alter in the future.

SIGNS OF A SOUND SUBFLOOR

A good subfloor should exhibit the following key attributes:

Able to take existing and additional loads

If the floor gives underfoot, call in a contractor or structural engineer for advice.

Moisture free

Danger signs of moisture include smell, stains or soft spots.

Well insulated

Old houses often have uninsulated ground floors that leak air and heat. Noise between floors can also be intrusive. These problems must be rectified before further work is carried out.

Flat and even

Uneven floors are often a sign of structural problems and make the addition of floor coverings more difficult.

Floor coverings

Whether you need a further floor covering over the subfloor depends not only on how you are going to use each room but also on how you wish to live. Practical issues include cost, waterproofing, amount of maintenance, noise reduction and safety. Color and warmth, softness and comfort, and the ability to change with time are also considerations.

Whether you choose wood, stone, carpets, natural fibers or linoleum, ask your supplier for details to ensure that the material comes from a sustainable, eco-friendly source. The real environmental impact of flooring also comes after it is installed, so before buying make sure that it can be maintained with eco-friendly cleaning products (see page 164); it will age well; and it can be reused, recycled or disposed of responsibly.

WOOD
Wood can be the best flooring material for your eco-home

because it is naturally renewable, long lasting, attractive and healthy, and can be grown locally. Forests also provide habitats for most of the earth's plants and animals, create oxygen, store water and carbon, are home to some of the oldest human communities and give us some of the world's most stunning landscapes. Forests are

also a source of natural medicines, an economic resource for those who live in less industrialized societies and a critical part of our planet's climatic regulation.

Wood flooring comes in many forms, ranging from thick planks of American red oak and Scandinavian birch plywood panels to rich teak parquet and

> smooth and sleek
Not only is wood flooring an attractive, eco-friendly option, it is also warm under-foot and easy to clean. Lighter-colored woods, such as maple, beech and birch, reflect sunlight, brightening the room.

cork tiles from the bark of Portuguese oaks. While these are examples of wood from well-managed sources, very few of the many varieties sold around the world are grown and replaced carefully. Green guides to eco-woods exclude all but three tropical hardwoods—teak, rubberwood and greenheart—of which only the hard-wearing teak is suitable for flooring. Even then, very few teak plantations are managed well, so choose carefully.

When selecting wood, it is often best to choose woods grown in the temperate world. Since Europe has the most well-established woodland conservation program, wood from Europe is a good bet, although careful forest management is now spreading worldwide. The most credible wood-labeling program was set up by the Forest Stewardship Council (FSC), a global organization that ensures not only that wood sources are continuously replenished, but also that the rights of the local people and workers are protected. Further, it aims to complement natural forests by retaining old-growth wilderness and conserving biodiversity. Look for the FSC logo when choosing your wood.

The right type of wood

Woods are divided botanically. Softwoods are produced by coniferous trees, such as pines, while hardwoods are produced by broad-leaved trees, such as oak. Unfortunately, some hardwoods are soft and some softwoods are hard! Floors need to be durable and woods used in wet or humid environments need to be resistant to rot. Temperate hardwoods suitable for flooring range from pale birch and beech to darker woods such as jarrah, oak and chestnut. Softwood flooring like fir, pine and European redwood are often faster growing and cheaper. Better still, choose reclaimed (that is, secondhand) wood, which is beautiful, seasoned and full of character, making it a very good eco-choice. Salvage and reclamation yards are plentiful and often have a wide range of interesting reclaimed woods at good prices.

Wood panel systems

Solid wood floors can be expensive, so many people choose composite wood panels, such as plywood, chipboard and MDF (medium density fiberboard), as cheap alternatives. Most of these panels are made from waste wood chippings, which, in principle, is an environmentally sound process. In practice, however, the source of the wood may not be sustainable. Also, many panels are bonded together with chemical resins that are definitely toxic and have been linked to allergies. This is not to

∧ **parquet perfection**
Traditionally laid by skilled craftspeople, parquet flooring is very stylish, hard wearing and long lasting.

ECO-TIP

Protecting wooden floors
Waxes and varnishes will protect most woods from staining and damage. Beeswax protects most interior woods, but you can also buy solid oil varnishes, which are low in solvents and contain a variety of natural raw materials, such as linseed, sunflower, soybean and thistle oil, together with plant waxes. Interior woods don't need preservative treatments, many of which are harmful, but they do need water protection. Wood also needs plenty of air circulating around it to prevent moisture from building up and causing rot. Avoid synthetic varnishes, such as polyurethanes, because these can cause skin irritation or allergic reactions.

∧ **completely floored**
There is a huge variety of floor coverings available for your home, each with its own merits and shortcomings. These include (clockwise from top left) carpets, stone tiles, rugs and Ttura, a type of terrazzo sold in Europe. When deciding which one to choose, consider its suitability to the function of the room in question.

say that all board products are dangerous. Plywood is probably the least toxic board material available and also the most attractive. Make sure that it comes from a truly sustainable source and that the level of formaldehyde, a toxic resin used in the manufacture of wood panels, is listed as "low" on the label.

HEAVY MATERIALS

Full of ecological contradictions, heavy flooring options are often misunderstood and misused. From a positive point of view, we will never run out of stone, sand, clay and gravel. Also, floors made from these materials need next to no maintenance over their long life because they are easy to clean and hypoallergenic. In warm climates, a shaded and well-ventilated room with a stone or concrete floor will remain cooler in the heat of the day, while in cold climates, a heavy floor placed to catch the low winter sun will retain its heat long after night has settled in.

Yet floors made from stone, concrete or ceramics do consume considerable energy in their manufacture. Open-cast quarries degrade the landscape and often provide poorly paid and dangerous work. Transporting and machining heavy stone consumes vast quantities of fuel, as does firing cement and clay to make concrete and tiles. Using heavy flooring may also entail making some structural modifications (such as larger foundations) to your home. Finally, concrete is considered the devil incarnate by some, with the vast majority of concrete buildings constructed in the last fifty years being ugly, dehumanizing and often technically flawed.

To really benefit from these materials, you need to use them selectively. Restrict them to certain areas of the home such as the ground floor, where they will not be too heavy. They are also good for highly trafficked areas such as thresholds, hearths and kitchens, and they can also provide a waterproof surface in bathrooms. If these materials are used in a ventilated pantry, food will be kept naturally cooler.

Stone

Ranging from smooth marble to rough-hewn granite, stone is usually laid on a layer of cement on a concrete subfloor. Choose local stones that are in plentiful supply, from quarries that have strong environmental policies. These stones will not only be more ecological but will also enhance your region's character and provide local employment. In the United Kingdom, for example, Welsh slate and limestone from the Cotswolds are better choices than Italian marble or cheaper South American slates.

Ceramics

Made from fired clay, ceramic tiles do cause environmental pollution even though the raw material is fairly unlimited. Tiles that contain recycled glass are more ecological. Ceramic floors are best restricted to areas where waterproof surfaces are helpful, such as in bathrooms or around kitchen sinks. Ceramic tiles are hard to attach to wooden subfloors because they do not expand and contract at the same rate as the wood underneath; in these instances, choose flexible flooring instead, such as linoleum or rubber. Also, avoid glass and polished tiles on floors because they are very slippery when wet.

Tiles are regionally specific, despite worldwide marketing by manufacturers. Try to choose local tiles from small workshops that create beautiful objects with depth, texture and individual color.

Terrazzo

This hard-wearing and waterproof flooring material is made from cement, sand and stone, or glass chippings. Available in tile form, or poured and polished on site, terrazzo lasts indefinitely and can be polished to a very elegant sheen year after year. Some forms of terrazzo are made with an epoxy resin in place of cement. One such material, marketed in Europe as Ttura, is particularly

> encouraging warmth

Laying down stone floors in the conservatory or another room that gets plenty of sun has the benefit of storing warmth for the whole house, which will also help to reduce your heating bills.

eco-friendly, being made from 85 percent recycled glass and nonsolvinated epoxy resins.

Brick

Hard-wearing but difficult to keep clean, brick floors are best used in areas that don't need to be kept spotless, such as hallways and work rooms. The manufacture of bricks is more energy-consuming than that of concrete products, so it's best to make use of reclaimed stock, which can be bought from salvage yards in many colors, ranging from rich browns to hard blues.

CARPETS AND RUGS

Fabric floor coverings have been made for many thousands of years and, although now ubiquitous, were once considered a luxury. Woven by hand with threads colored by carefully chosen natural dyes, they were lain over earth, wood or stone floors to provide warmth, comfort and enchantment. Over the centuries, each local region developed its own style, sometimes abstract, sometimes figurative. The invention of the automated loom created a revolution in the production of textiles, and a carpet that once might have been made in a week can now be woven in a few hours. The automated loom's insatiable demand for raw materials has led to the worldwide market for wool and cotton and the development of artificial fibers such as nylon and acrylic. It has also created one-dimensional products with no sign of human contact, each knot identical, and each color completely uniform and consistent.

If you have a choice, rugs are a better eco-option for your home than fitted carpets. Rugs can be taken outside to be aired and beaten, removing the need for continuous vacuum cleaning and reducing the problem of house dust mites and other allergens. They can also be taken with you when you move to another home.

Fitted carpets, on the other hand, run under furniture, making them far harder to clean. They also require specialist equipment such as carpet shampoo. Although they appear to provide a versatile complement to modern furniture layout, the truth is that areas in the sun will eventually change color. Well-trodden areas will lose their pile quickly and carpets placed under heavy furniture will eventually compress, requiring early replacement. Furthermore, carpets and their underlay give off polluting gases and the carpet fibers can trap toxins brought in from the street on shoes. >

Eternally yours: rugs

Small, brightly colored rugs on a timber floor are a far better ecological option than wall-to-wall carpets. Not only are they easy to clean and provide warmth and comfort, but they also age with us and are easy to take along when we move. Choose well-made wool, silk or cotton rugs that have been colored with natural dyes.

Tatami mats

Filled with densely packed straw and covered with a
thin layer of more finely woven matting, rice straw slabs
are the key ingredient in traditional Japanese flooring.
Tatami mats are 2 to 2¾ inches thick and slightly under 3¼ feet in width and 6½ feet
in length. They are edged along the long sides with narrow strips of black linen and
lain in a counterclockwise spiral from the center of a room. The mat forms the basic
unit around which rooms and homes were built—eight mats for the living space and
six mats for the dining room. In Japan today, studio and apartment dimensions are
still described by the number of tatami mats they contain. The covering layer should
be replaced every three or four years. If you choose tatami mats for part of your
home, try to make it a shoe-free zone, since they are not hard wearing.

> Ensuring that your carpeting has felt underlay made from recycled fabrics or wool sources with hessian backing, and not the more toxic polyurethane or rubber underlay, is a more eco-friendly gesture. Even so, many carpets are chemically treated to reduce staining and water damage, which can cause allergic reactions. If you opt for carpets, introduce a "no-shoes" policy in your home, air rooms once a week and vacuum regularly to remove bugs and dust.

The best textiles

The best fibers for floor coverings are natural ones like wool, cotton and silk. Wool carpets are usually made from sheep's wool, which is soft, springy and long lasting. It is a texture that holds dye well and provides warmth and good sound insulation. Even so, the wool industry does cause some pollution due to the chemicals used in sheep dips, the dyes used to color the products and the fire retardants used to treat them.

Cotton rugs, such as kilims from Turkey, provide a lighter alternative to wool rugs. They are not as tough or long lasting, however, and are best used in areas that are subject to less wear, such as bedrooms. They are good to have in bathrooms because they can soak up any water that spills on the floor, and then be hung outside to dry.

Silk is produced by the silk worm, which lives in China and feeds exclusively on mulberry leaves. These worms are farmed by the millions and killed for the fine, soft and exceedingly strong thread that is then dyed and woven to create tightly knotted and very soft carpets. Since the knots are extremely small, silk carpets are very long lasting but expensive and are best used as a small decoration rather than a wall-to-wall luxury.

Synthetic carpets are not as soft, durable or environmentally sound as wool carpets, but they are cheaper. Nylon, polypropylene and acrylics are the most extensively used synthetics, but, although they are available in a huge range of colors and styles, I do not recommend them. Nylon, for example, is responsible for the release of the greenhouse gas nitrous oxide, which also contributes to ozone depletion and forms acid rain. Synthetic carpets are made from a variety of petro-chemically derived fibers that use high-energy processes and produce many toxins over their life.

> **naturally trendy**
Natural fabrics, such as (top to bottom) sisal, sea grass, coir and jute, have become very popular in recent times. Although they are attractive and have good eco-credentials, they are not very long lasting and suffer from water damage and general wear and tear.

OTHER NATURAL FIBERS

The range of natural fibers available for floor covering has grown enormously in recent years as we have realized the enormous benefits of simple, biodegradable and healthy materials.

While each type of natural fiber has its own particular quality, they are all generally suitable for less trafficked areas but should be used with a no-shoes policy since they are particularly hard to keep clean. They are all quite abrasive under foot and you may wish to avoid them if you have small children.

Sea grass

Grown in seawater paddy fields in China, sea grass forms part of nature's tidal defenses, protecting and enhancing mangrove swamps and reefs. It is handwoven in a variety of decorative patterns and is naturally stain resistant (which also means that it can't be dyed). Modern and muted, sea grass is a popular choice in many homes, but bear in mind that it isn't a suitable material for stairs, where it can become slippery underfoot.

Hemp

Made from the cannabis plant, this has been used for a whole range of natural products. The earliest known use was in Southeast Asia more than 6,000 years ago and until the middle of the twentieth century it was considered a great low-cost crop with thousands of applications ranging from fabrics and sealants to wall insulation. Antimarijuana legislation stopped most commercial production, and only recently have hemp-based products, including floor matting, been reintroduced. Some people believe that the widespread use of hemp could dramatically reduce the use of other, more toxic, materials.

Coir

A waste product from coconut farming, coir is made from the nut's outer husk, which is first softened for up to a year in lagoons and then woven to produce a very hard-wearing mat. Popularly used outside the front door, it is also suitable indoors throughout the home. Although it is basically a good green product, some of the estuaries have been polluted by the sheer volume of matting left to soften in them and this has adversely affected the local aquatic life.

Sisal

Grown from the grass stems of the sisalana bush in Africa and South America, this material is soft enough for bedrooms and tough enough to withstand chair legs in living and dining rooms.

∨ **simple and chic**
More practical than carpet, sisal is a good choice for your dining room. The strong weave means that it won't decompress under the weight of seated diners.

Bamboo

This is the fastest growing plant on the earth. Resin-impregnated bamboo floorboards are tough, easy to clean and available in a variety of widths and stains to suit living rooms and kitchens alike.

Jute

Long-stemmed plants around the Ganges Delta in Bangladesh provide the raw material for jute. It is mainly used in the production of hessian, but it is also available in a soft (and consequently short-lived) weave.

LINOLEUM, RUBBER AND SYNTHETICS

Resilient and smooth floor coverings are relatively modern and the cheapest waterproof and easily cleaned surface. Vinyl tiles or sheets are the most common smooth flooring. These are available in any color, easy to fix, very cheap and often designed to mimic natural floorings. Unfortunately they are manufactured from polyvinyl chloride (PVC), combined with fungicides, pigments and plasticizers, so they are not the most eco-friendly of materials.

Linoleum is as inexpensive as vinyl, but it lasts longer and has better eco-credentials. It is made from mainly renewable and natural ingredients, chiefly linseed oil and natural resins mixed with cork, ground stone powder and wood flour, which are heat-bound onto a hessian backing. Not only are the resulting linoleum tiles safe, but they have also been shown to kill harmful bacteria. However, the raw materials often need to be transported a very long distance to reach their place of manufacture.

Many linoleum products are sold with a marbled effect slightly reminiscent of school corridor floors. There is a growing range of single-color tiles, however, that is much more modern. Always remember to use the natural adhesive called lignin paste to stick linoleum tiles down onto the floor rather than more toxic solvent-based glues.

Rubber is an alternative resilient material that is long lasting and relatively benign. It does not contain plasticizers or heavy metals and one manufacturer claims that all their ingredients are eco-compatible and nontoxic.

Most rubber floors are made from artificial rubber with minimal natural latex. They are available in a wide range of colors and textures, but the flat and plain options are easier to clean and will last through more fashion changes than the dimpled, exotically colored alternatives.

< alternative style
Modern designs have elevated the no-nonsense linoleum tile to a stylish yet eco-friendly flooring option.

Walls represent more surface area than any other surface in a home—four in each room, two sides to each wall, plus interior and exterior walls, load-bearing walls, window walls and stud partitions. Walls frame spaces; act as boundaries; reflect and diffuse light; provide color, hide wiring; and carry doors, windows and shelving. Sometimes we wish there were more walls in our home, to create a playroom, study or second bathroom. At other times we crave more space and fewer rooms. Adding and removing walls is not a simple undertaking, but it is far easier than moving to a new house, and it will certainly rejuvenate your home.

LOAD-BEARING WALLS

Made from brick or concrete, these create solid barriers between rooms and often support the floor above. They are hard to move but, like concrete floors, provide solidity, thermal stability and good acoustic separation between the spaces in your home.

Solid walls make electrical modifications difficult because routes for conduits need to be chased out and rerendered. Also, they should never be

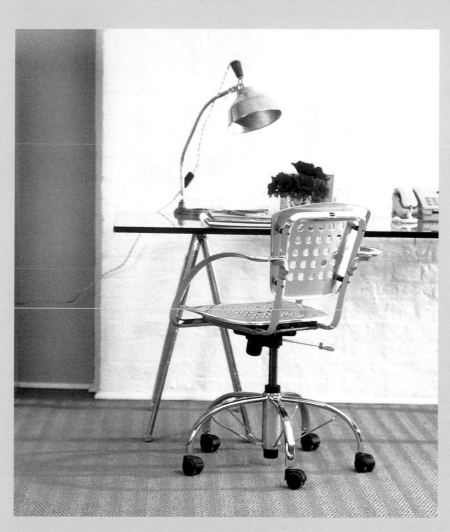

∧ the rough and the smooth

A couple of coats of paint will immediately transform a bare brick wall. Alternatively, you can render it with plaster to create a smoother surface that can be decorated with a wall finish of your choice or simply left bare.

removed without the advice of a building contractor or engineer since they might be supporting the floor above!

STUD-WORK WALLS

These are made from vertical and horizontal wood elements braced by floors and external walls. The studs are covered with plasterboard panels and the space between the boards is used to run electrical cables and stuffed with sound absorbing insulation. They use far less material than load-bearing walls and are easier to modify for new wiring or new doors. Some stud walls do support floors above so, as with any walls, it is always best to check with a contractor or engineer before you undertake to remove them.

TECHNOLOGY

Stud-work walls

Made from light wood frames, stud-work walls are often used in modern houses and conversions.

Much easier and cheaper to build than the more solid brick walls, their eco-credentials can be maximized by filling the space between the two panels with mineral fiber or cellulose insulation material to increase the thermal and acoustic separation between rooms. You can also build storage spaces into stud-work walls, creating thick walls that make a pleasant transition between spaces.

horizontal wood beam

insulation

skirting

wood joists

floor boards

If you are building new internal walls, then stud work provides the quickest, most flexible solution. Instead of building thin walls, consider constructing each wall with a wide storage space that can be accessed from either side and modified to suit your changing needs. Always check with your local building authority first to see whether you need permission to build or remove walls.

WALL COVERINGS

Once you have a clean and flat wall, you can then decide how to decorate it. The typical considerations are color and feel, maintenance and wear resistance. However, you should also consider how the walls will reflect and spread light, how their color affects the warmth and size of rooms and how walls fit with other finishes, artworks and furniture in your home.

Eco-friendly paints

One of the cheapest and quickest ways to transform a room is to paint its walls a new color. But walls do not stand apart from the rest of your furniture and finishes, and it is always best to be as careful in your choice of paint as you are in your choice of other home furnishings.

The chief differences between the various paints lie in their toxicity, durability, color and sheen. Perhaps it's not surprising, but most of us spend far too much time agonizing over the color and far too little wondering about its effect on our health. The majority of paints available today are derived from the petrochemical industry, using synthetic dyes for color and a rich and toxic mix of solvents, binders, emulsifiers, fillers, thinners and drying agents. It's no wonder that painting is officially recognized as a dangerous and unhealthy trade.

Synthetic paints

If you do use these, avoid high-sheen water-based paints and all solvent-based paints inside the home, because they give off high levels of toxic volatile compounds. Low-sheen water-based paints are still toxic but emit less than a fifth of the chemicals associated with other synthetics. In all cases, while you are painting, ensure that the room is well ventilated and that any doors between this room and the rest of your home are closed. Don't use the room until the paint is completely dry and all traces of odor are gone. Paints are now being labeled with health warnings that indicate the amount of volatile organic compounds (VOC) they contain, so read the label carefully to ensure that VOC levels are low. Better still, choose natural paints that contain only healthy ingredients, such as chalk, linseed oil, earth pigments, beeswax, talcum powder and harvested tree resins.

CLOSE-UP: PAINT PIGMENTS

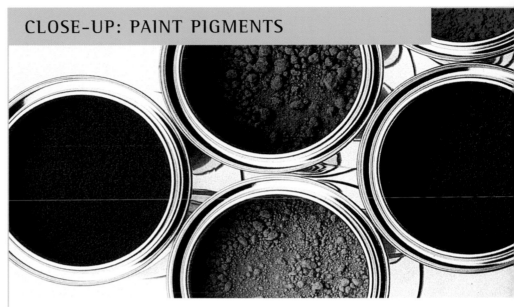

Some paints can be purchased without added color so that you can create your own hues from natural pigments. Earth pigments include oxides of iron (which are red to brown), ochres, umbers and grays. Richer colors can be obtained from mineral pigments extracted from the ground, cleaned and milled. Some of these are also heat-treated to create different colors. You can mix pigments together if you can't find the color you like, but be aware that these natural pigments are not generally as intense as commercial dyes. Certain types consist of more intense pigments derived from the chemical industry. These aren't as eco-friendly as the natural ones but, all things considered, don't rule out a bright-colored wall if you think it'll look great in your home!

Plant-based paints, waxes and varnishes

These are available in a wide range of colors and textures in specialist shops, in some mainstream DIY stores or direct from the manufacturers. They are suitable for internal and external painting on plaster, wood and metal surfaces and pose minimal health hazards. Some natural paints take longer to dry than synthetic ones do, but they are less toxic so the rooms can be used straight after painting. Plant-based paints are also microporous, which means that

> design tools

Once you've got the knack, wallpaper is relatively simple to hang and will mask minor bumps and holes in wall surfaces.

although they are water-resistant, they still allow water vapor to flow through the wall, which helps to prevent the paint from blistering.

Alternative indoor paints

Distemper is a traditional paint made from chalk and linseed oil binder. It can be wiped clean but isn't suitable in areas that are easily marked, such as in children's bedrooms or hallways.

Casein paints are made from distemper bound with a milk by-product. The casein helps to bind and seal the paint, making it washable and longer lasting.

Wall surfaces can also be given depth and texture by rendering with fine clay or adding mineral powder to the paint mixture. Natural paints are often provided in powder form for mixing with water at your home. Natural resin emulsion paints look and behave just like commercial emulsions but don't contain harmful ingredients.

If you are decorating outside walls or painting directly onto plaster or cement, then you can use mineral paints that are manufactured from water glass (potassium silicate) and inorganic color pigments. This type of paint actually binds deep into the cement base to create a colored surface that is durable, colorfast and easily cleaned. It is odorless and nontoxic and allows the wall to breathe. Potassium silicate can also be used directly with water to prime loose and dusty wall surfaces or can be mixed with natural pigments to create a color wash glaze.

Wallpaper

Covering walls with printed paper provides instant color, texture, pattern, and a wipe-clean surface. Wallpapers range from thick lining papers designed to cover uneven walls to highly decorated, hand-finished papers and mass-produced textured vinyl.

Wallpaper is a good environmental material since its chief ingredient is wood pulp, which is produced in a sustainable manner or comes from recycled sources. You also need only a small amount of wallpaper to cover a wall. The print dyes found in wallpaper generally come from the chemical industry, but it is possible to find some wallpapers hand-printed with natural dyes. Alternatively, you can simply buy plain lining and decorate it yourself with natural paints. Wallpaper also has the advantage of providing a quick way to hide an uneven wall surface.

Paper is used as the backing for a variety of natural materials, including cork, hessian and raffia, that can be hung on walls. The paper makes it easier to hang these materials, which you can mix and match to create changing textures and colors on a wall.

It is also possible to purchase vinyl wallpaper, which is basically paper covered in a thin film of PVC. This type of wallpaper is often used in wet environments, such as bathrooms and utility rooms, because it resists water and can be easily wiped clean. While the amount of vinyl used is relatively small, the ideal eco-home should not have it, not least because vinyl paper is one of the most unattractive finishes imaginable!

Wood paneling

Walls that are paneled with wood provide a soft and warm alternative to other types of wall coverings. Use tongue-and-groove solid wood panels and treat them with natural waxes, oils or colored varnishes. Vary the look by hanging strips vertically or horizontally or by choosing wide planks instead of the usual narrow boards. Alternatively, use large plywood panels to create a modern wall that can incorporate hidden electrical outlets and storage space behind a smooth and semireflective surface. Because wood paneling doesn't take heavy loads and water

damage is unlikely, choose softer woods like pine, a good and cheap choice. You can also use cork tiles for additional heat and noise insulation.

Tiles

Made from fired clay or glass, tiles come in all sizes, colors and

prices and are a long-lasting, maintenance-free and water-resistant option for covering your walls. Small tiles are now sold on backing sheets of hessian or paper, allowing you to fix large quantities quickly and accurately. Ceramic tiles are opaque and are usually glazed for protection. Unglazed tiles

∧ **wall to wall**
The huge array of wall coverings leaves you spoiled for choices when you are decorating your home. They include (clockwise from top left) large stone tiles, painted wood paneling, metal wall finishes and mosaic ceramic tiles.

∧ glass bricks
Create an internal wall or partition using glass bricks. Use them sparingly to lighten rooms that have poor access to natural light.

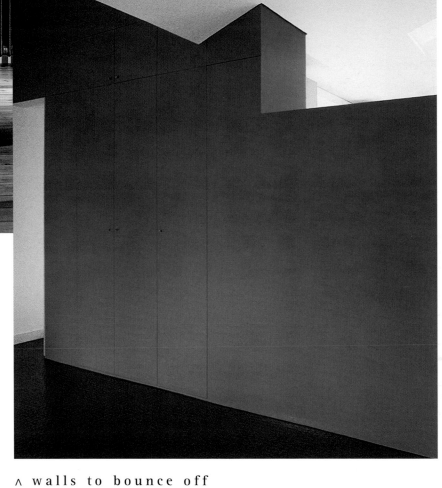

∧ walls to bounce off
Rubber sheets can also be used on walls. They make a tough, long-lasting alternative to ceramics, particularly in rooms that get wet.

need to be waxed like wood and will age gently over time. Glass tiles add sparkle to wall finishes and are generally more expensive. Tiles can be laid in a huge number of imaginative patterns. They are best used in wet environments, around baths and showers and in kitchens, and they work equally well on vertical and horizontal surfaces.

Tiles consume more energy and materials in their manufacture than paper or paint do, so it is best to limit their use to areas that will benefit from water resistance.

Metal wall finishes
Walls of aluminum, stainless steel or copper sheeting have recently become fashionable, and, although these are considered "minimal" in the world of interior design, they are actually "maximal" in ecological terms. To produce aluminum, for example, bauxite needs to be dug out from the side of a mountain, a whole region has to be flooded to build a hydroelectric dam and the manufactured sheets of metal then need to be shipped around the world.

If you must have metal wall finishes, limit them to small areas of your home and use stainless steel in preference to other metals. Consider installing a small square of polished beaten copper plate in the center of an unplastered wall so the reflecting copper becomes a shimmering piece of art instead of an expensive and environmentally destructive decorative foil.

Few of us have the opportunity to construct our homes from scratch, but maybe once in our lives we are lucky enough to build an extension or convert an attic.

THE ROOF

Possibly the most critical part of the home, the roof protects the rest of your home from the effects of the weather and may enable you to collect natural resources for reuse. If you are moving to a new house, look for pitched or sloping roofs since these shed rain quickly and are easier to maintain than flat roofs. Flat roofs also have to take the weight of snow and so are not advisable if you live in a cold climate. You also need to consider the use of the space underneath the roof. In places where land is at a premium, a loft makes inexpensive real estate, so aim to design the roof structure for living space rather than storage. Avoid closely spaced gang-nail trusses, which are cheaper but fill the attic space with structure, and choose wider wood beams and rafters supported on vertical columns instead. Placing insulation directly under the roof plane between joists will ensure that the roof space is ready for occupation when you need it.

On pitched roofs, wood shingles or thatch are the most benign covering since they require little energy to make. However, there are few regions in the industrialized world where these sorts of roofs are still commonly used, they require careful maintenance, and they pose a fire hazard. Concrete tiles use less energy than traditional clay or slate tiles but they are still being made to mimic other materials rather than expressing their own nature, which seems a shame. Of the metal roofing options, only

< green tops
If you're building or repairing a flat roof, consider a turf covering. As well as being attractive and self-maintaining, it will also provide a home for birds.

recycled stainless-steel sheeting offers a low-energy, low-maintenance and nontoxic roof covering. If you opt for metal roofing, avoid lead, copper and zinc since these cause damage to water-borne animals.

If your home has a flat roof or you are planning to design a flat roof for an extension, it should ideally be made from softwood joists and panels because these are low-energy renewable materials. Consider covering it with a shallow layer of earth in which you can plant grasses. This provides an alternative sunbathing terrace that will attract birds, insects and other flora and fauna found in a conventional garden. To make the roof waterproof, use EPDM elastomeric sheeting and cork or expanded polystyrene for insulation under the earth layer. Slope the roof by an angle of more than three degrees in order to prevent water buildup on the roof surface. Before undertaking such a project, however, consult your local building authority to make sure your plan meets local building codes.

WINDOWS

Single-glazed windows are good at letting light in but they also let heat out. It is therefore essential that you choose double-glazed window units; you'll save even more energy if you install low-e double glazing or triple glazing, particularly if you live in a cool climate. A typical home needs no more than 20 to 30 percent of its wall surface glazed in order to be brightly lit by the sun during the day and retain its heat at night. Use larger windows on sun-facing walls and smaller ones on shady façades.

Wood window frames protected by plant-based paints are twice the price of vinyl window frames, but they are more beautiful and, if properly maintained, last longer. An even better option is water-resistant wood, such as tough European oak and hemlock. Overhanging eaves will also protect windows from driving rain. Metal frames made from aluminum need more energy to construct than wood frames do, but they are easier to maintain. No matter what material you decide on for your window

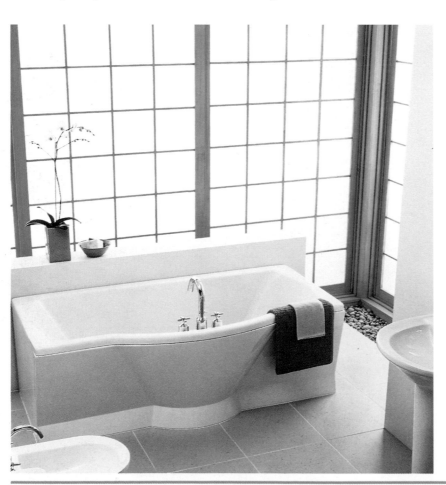

< style and function
Bathrooms built next to an exterior wall allow for natural ventilation. Opaque glass replaces paper tiles in this distinctly Japanese-style bathroom, allowing the wall to serve as a window, too.

frames, they all need to be repainted or protected after the first five or ten years.

Another element to consider in your choice of window is how it opens. Side-hung windows are easy to open and close to a tight seal in winter, while sash windows are more prone to failure. Avoid top or center-hung windows since these will provide only a small opening in summer or intrude in the room when open fully.

If you live in a warm climate, choose inward opening or sash windows with shutters so that you can close external louvres for shade and security on hot days, but maintain a cooling breeze.

DOORS

Like windows, doors should provide an airtight seal for comfort during winter. The best designs incorporate weatherproofing and are made with insulated wood paneling or low-e double-glazed windows.

EXTERNAL WALLS

The cost of a wood-framed home is similar to that of a brick home, and both last for an equally long time if properly maintained.

An interesting alternative to wood framing is to construct an extension to your home from a frame that is made of recycled steel, which is then protected in stainless-steel profiled cladding (again, recycled). This system is commonly used for industrial warehouses, but a good architect might be able to create something quite special on a domestic scale.

The reason for stainless steel's good eco-credentials is the fact that a wood cladding system will need maintenance and repair every five to ten years, whereas stainless-steel cladding will need very little.

The final key to an ecologically correct wall is the generous use of insulation as discussed in chapter 2. Choose cellulose fiber for a wood frame and rock or fiberglass wool for a load-bearing cavity wall and ensure that you use at least 6 inches, if not more, to keep your home cozy through cold winter nights and cool during hot summer days.

Furnishings and fixtures

It is only when we pack up our things to move to a new home and the delivery van slowly fills with sofas, tables, lamps and bookcases that we realize how many possessions we have accumulated over the years. At times like these we may find ourselves wondering how we ever decided to buy that coffee table, cushion or whatnot. Often the reasons are clouded in time, but the truth is that we are easily persuaded by instant appeal and cost. We are never really given much information about where a product comes from, what it is made out of or how long it will last.

Some companies are beginning to make a move in the right direction but there is no clear guide to whether the furniture we choose is environmentally friendly.

One way to assess this is by thinking in the long term before you buy. Imagine whether you will still like the piece in twenty years' time. Check, too, that it is well made so that it will actually last this long. If there is no manufacturer information on testing, then sit on furniture and lift it up to see if it's been designed for the real world. Ask the retailer what it is made from and where it was manufactured. If you have a choice, go for low-energy or recycled goods that are made locally over high-energy foreign imports. Consider multifunctional, adaptable and portable furniture that you can use in a variety of ways as time goes by.

While wood is usually a good bet, don't forget that recycled glass and metal often make beautiful objects too. You should also accept that plastic, for all its faults, is a material that can be transformed into cheap, long-lasting and funky products, provided that designers and

∧ **multifunctional**
Try to choose furniture that has dual functions, as well as being made from sustainable resources. A futon sofa, for example, transforms into a spare bed.

suits you
Whether you prefer a country-house style (above) or a modern, minimalist look (right), an eco-friendly home is one that allows you to express your individual tastes.

manufacturers understand and respect its qualities of lightness, strength and translucency.

WOOD FURNITURE

If you're contemplating purchasing tables and chairs, the likelihood is that you are probably looking at wood, whether you are interested in a traditional style with well-turned legs and inlaid veneers, or a more modern design.

People tend to spend a lot of time and money choosing wooden furniture, yet how many stop to think where the wood comes from and what might have become of its forest home and the wildlife? The same basic guidelines for choosing wood for flooring and other decorative purposes apply to buying wood furniture, although wood used for furniture is generally either exposed and hard wearing or hidden, low grade and simple.

Solid wood furniture can be a delight, aging well and traveling with you through your life. Make sure that the wood is sourced from sustainable forests and avoid delicate frames or thin veneers that are easily broken. Once you have made your purchase, treat the wood with care, waxing it regularly and wiping off water stains as quickly as you can. If you have the choice, choose solid wood over a wood veneer because a wood surface can always be resanded and finished should it deteriorate, while veneers are very hard to replace.

Low-grade wood is often used to frame sofas and beds. The problem with this wood is not that it comes from fast-disappearing native forests, but that it is designed for a short life and often contains mildly toxic chemicals.

When choosing sofas and other covered furnishings, always lift up the skirt and have a good look at the supports and joints underneath. Wooden furniture should be held together with strong wood joints or good metal brackets and bolts, rather than staples and glue. Poor-quality furniture often looks fine when first purchased, but it can be easily damaged when you start to move it around at home. Choose solid woods or plywood in preference to chipboard covered with melamine or veneers (look for the Forest Stewardship Council mark on labels). If you do use chipboard, always choose those with a low formaldehyde content, since they will not pollute your home. For more information on pollutants found in the home, see page 165.

METALS

Although beautiful, long lasting and relatively easy to recycle, metals are also rare, often toxic and require intensive energy to extract. According to the World Resource Institute, we will run out of metals that can be mined in less than one hundred years, with the exceptions of nickel, iron and aluminum. What's more, the energy required to mine 2.2 pounds of iron is thirty times greater than the energy required to harvest 2.2 pounds of wood: and aluminum requires one hundred times as much energy as wood does! Natural habitats are often destroyed by the huge quantities of material that are moved to extract metal.

If you do choose to furnish your home with metals, you should think of these items as precious, treating them like jewelry for your home. A general principle is to use wood for larger items and metal for smaller ones. Instead of covering your kitchen with stainless steel, for instance, use metal as a focal point in your design—a stunning candleholder or an elegant copper trim set into the top of a dark elm coffee table.

Aluminum

This very light and strong metal is extracted from bauxite ore in a

METALS AND THEIR YEARS UNTIL EXHAUSTION

Once used for ornament and tools, metals are now regularly thrown away. If we use them in our homes, we should treat them like a piece of precious jewelry.

Metal ore	Years remaining
Gold	30
Silver	30
Lead	45
Zinc	50
Cadmium	50
Tin	55
Copper	60
Mercury	80
Nickel	120
Iron	230
Bauxite	260
Uranium	410
Manganese ore	685

> iron everywhere

You may not realize it, but iron and its alloys have a place in every part of your home. From top to bottom: cast iron can be used to make coat hooks, galvanized steel is suitable for wall cabinets, brushed steel is used to make cooking vessels and chrome-plated steel makes a long-lasting hook for keys.

process requiring huge inputs of electricity. Fortunately, much of this energy is created using hydro-electric power, which is a renewable resource. Yet the resulting loss of natural habitat, toxic spoils and secondary emissions make excess use of aluminum a bad thing.

Aluminum can be used all over the home and, being lightweight and easy to store, has become a popular alternative for window frames, garden furniture, guttering and curved roofing. Since aluminum degrades in acidic rain, much of it is powder coated, which makes recycling impossible. This is unfortunate because unadulterated aluminum is easy and cheap to reuse. Inside the home, aluminum retains a dull light gray sheen that is chic and modern. Instead of using aluminum panels to cover walls and floors, reserve it for detail— high-quality metal work, storage containers, picture frames and light fixtures.

Copper

This soft, dull reddish-gold metal fades to green as it weathers. It is a high-energy product with less than one hundred years left in the ground and its extraction from mines causes huge amounts of pollution. Over 50 percent of copper is recycled because of its high resale value.

Hand-beaten copperware has been used and valued for thousands of years and makes highly conductive cookware. Because copper oxide is toxic, make sure you clean cookware made from this material very well. Copper is also used around the home for water pipes and roof flashing, but because it is so scarce, use plastic or stainless steel for plumbing purposes and PVC or galvanized steel for guttering.

Iron and steel

The Iron Age heralded our transition from hunter-gatherers to farmers and communitarians. Closer to the present age, the use of iron helped to create the industrial revolution, giving us the strength necessary for steam engines, which then made bridges, skyscrapers and automobiles. We are now recycling over 70 percent of scrap iron, and the energy content of iron and steel (which is an alloy of iron) is lower than other metals.

Steel and iron rust when used, so they are normally plated, enameled, painted or galvanized to protect them from corrosion. These processes are harmful; the steel industry is responsible for the release of hormone-disrupting dioxins and other toxins. In the home, we often use stainless steel that is protected from corrosion by the addition of chromium. Traditional uses of steel include cutlery, kitchen equipment, countertops and bathroom paneling. Stainless steel is long lasting and easy to clean and recycle. It makes a good choice for things in your home that will get wet.

Lead

In the past this soft, dark gray metal was used for roofing and plumbing, but it should not be used anywhere in the home because of its known toxic effects. If you have a very old house and are considering using rainwater from the roof as your supply of drinking water, make sure that all lead flashings have been replaced. Old paint may also contain lead, so if you are stripping any old paintwork be sure to wear a protective mask and long sleeves. Keep children and pregnant

Eternally yours: cutlery

A set of stainless-steel cutlery will last a lifetime, so consider your choice carefully. Because it is a very easy metal to work with, you will have lots of design options, ranging from the traditional to the modern. It is also lightweight, dishwasher safe, and water and stain resistant. Compared to silver it is relatively cheap and has better eco-credentials.

women out of the house until the stripping is done and any dust has been removed. Opening windows to create good ventilation and vacuuming with a HEPA-filter vacuum afterward are also good protective measures.

Zinc

With less than fifty years of reserves, this is another metal that is near the end of its life.

Zinc is generally used for galvanizing steel, but it has also found a niche as a fashionable finish for kitchen countertops in many modern homes. Since galvanized steel has a short life and the zinc coating is toxic to water-borne organisms, it is better to opt for stainless steel or a less energy-intensive material.

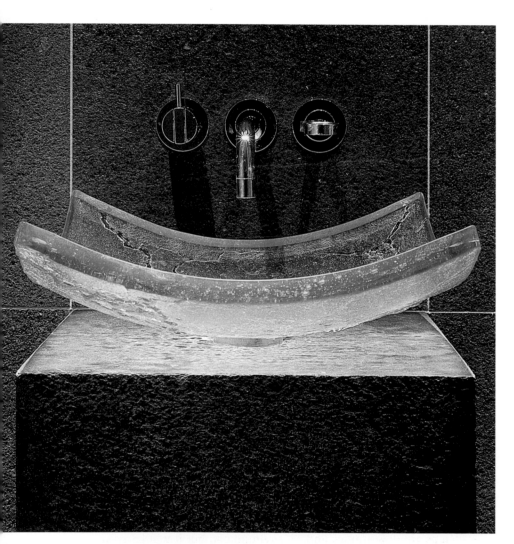

∧ **the beauty of glass**

Glass and water have a natural affinity, each capturing and reflecting light in their own way. Recycled glass with natural flaws makes a perfect container for flowers on a sunny window ledge, or it can be used more ambitiously and creatively, as is the case with this modern bathroom basin.

GLASS

Transparent or translucent, reflecting and refracting light, glass is like ice, frozen solid but still a liquid. It is made from sand, carbonates and sulphates, heated to 2730°F and then blown, spun or floated to produce glassware, glass fibers and window panes. It can be used in the home for spreading and diffusing light, or as an object of beauty in itself.

Many pieces of glassware are made from recycled sources, and you should choose these over more refined designs. Recycling glass reduces the need to extract more materials, reduces waste and cuts energy use by at least a tenth. Sea sand cannot be used for glass making, and the mining of silver sand continues to cause local environmental damage.

Glass can be easily recycled for most practical household uses, except for windows panes, which need to be made from uncontaminated glass in order to retain their strength.

Once formed, glass is nontoxic and airtight, making it ideal for storing foods and drink.

PLASTIC

Plastics are mainly derived from the oil industry and make up around 5 percent of the world's oil consumption. These materials are responsible for the release of large quantities of harmful toxins during their manufacture and are rarely recycled, resulting in growing mounds of complex waste. Some plastics are relatively simple, require little energy to make, release little pollution during their manufacture and are very easy to recycle. Polyethylene and polypropylene fall into this camp.

Polypropylene has found its way into our homes as a tough material for food storage containers and a cheap material for translucent mugs, waste bins and storage.

Polyethylene is generally used to make thin films for wrapping and bags. It is rarely recycled so it is best to use thicker reusable bags instead of thin throwaway ones. Try not to base the design of your home around an extensive use of plastic. Rather, find small plastic objects that complement a more natural surrounding.

PVC (or polyvinyl chloride) is on the hit list of many environmental organizations. While it is a low-energy consumer (it is made from salt and petroleum), its main disadvantage is the release of highly toxic dioxins that are created during manufacture and incineration. It is also mixed with plasticizers and heavy metals

∧ **poetic plastics**
Many companies have discovered that simple plastics, such as polypropylene, make refined and long-lasting objects, such as chairs, storage containers and jugs. These good uses of plastics around the home should be encouraged.

that are known to be toxic. Manufacturers are struggling hard to prove that both the additives and PVC itself are harmless and better for the environment than natural alternatives. Environmentally, PVC can only really be justified in situations where it is long lasting, such as in underground pipes. Even then, other plastics are just as strong and most environmentalists would recommend ceramics instead.

Most PVC products found in the home, such as window frames and garden furniture, are not attractive and age rather badly. It is much better to save up and buy something that adds value, as well as beauty, to your home.

Other synthetics found in the home include bitumen sheets (which are used for flat roofing), melamine (used as a water-resistant coating for tables and countertops), EPDM elastomers (also used for flat roofing and rubber seals), polyurethane (used in varnishes, sealants and roof sheeting) and polystyrene (used for insulation and lightweight packing materials). Natural alternatives such as cork, timber and coconut fibers are better for the environment, but it will be hard to avoid all use of synthetics in your home. Try to limit their use, however, and ask suppliers for alternative materials where possible.

Fabrics and fillings

Cushions, curtains, pillows, duvets, mattress fillings and soft furniture add color, texture and bounce to our surroundings. Without them, rooms can feel hard and clinical.

When you are choosing fabrics and fillings, factors to consider are the pollution created by the dyes and how the different fibers affect your health. While fabrics are generally fairly innocuous, a little thought can go a long way in helping to keep the planet clean.

NATURAL FIBERS

These are long-lasting, nontoxic and renewable materials that, when farmed well, contribute to healthy and vibrant country economies. Although sheep are dipped in harmful chemicals and cotton crops are sprayed with pesticides, natural materials still remain favorite fabrics for many green buyers because they breathe well, do not create static electricity and are relatively nonallergenic. Nevertheless, cotton is one of the most polluting crops on the planet, using 2 percent of all farmland and consuming a quarter of all pesticides. And, downstream from the cotton fields, huge quantities of synthetic dyes are used to color our cotton and wool.

Cotton

This has many uses around the home, from napkins and table-cloths to bedsheets and towels. Some growers are not only reducing the need for pesticides but also cross-breeding natural cottons to create a range of subtle colors from brown to mint green to pale pink, which need neither bleach, defoliants or dyes. If you can search out these cottons, you will be making a significant improvement to the environment. Look for organic labeling (Soil Association in the United Kingdom or Natural Cotton Colours, the U.S. growers of natural Acala Pima and soft Sea Island long-staple cotton).

Linen

Derived from the straw of the flax plant, linen ranges from cream to dark tan and grey. It is a good eco-material, being absorbent, colorfast and full of texture.

Wool

Wool products are heavier than other fabrics but are often longer lasting as well as better for the environment. Choose those materials that are naturally dyed and use them as throws or bedding to add warmth and color to your home.

tactile sensation
As well as color and style, the texture of fabrics you choose for your home will add to the overall mood you are aiming to create in each room.

Leather

This material can be extremely long lasting provided you choose a tough grade that is properly stitched and used on well-made furniture. However, the inhumane methods of production, particularly the slaughterhouse, taint leather's green image. The tanning process is also highly toxic and includes treatment with solvents and chemicals such as chromium sulphate.

To care for leather, use natural waxes to replenish the skin. Choose your leather furniture carefully so that you will treasure it for years to come. Avoid cheap leather suites that are not only poorly made but also exceedingly ugly.

SYNTHETIC FIBERS

Nylon, polyester and acrylic are the most common synthetic fibers found around the house and are used for fillings as well as fabrics. Although generally hard wearing, they attract dust and do not breathe as well as natural fibers do. Synthetic fibers cause less environmental damage than poorly grown cotton, but they are not as comfortable or as easy to clean. Renewable synthetics include rayon and acetate, which are made from wood waste.

Synthetic fillings are easier to wash than feather ones and are a good alternative for people who are allergic to feathers. Latex

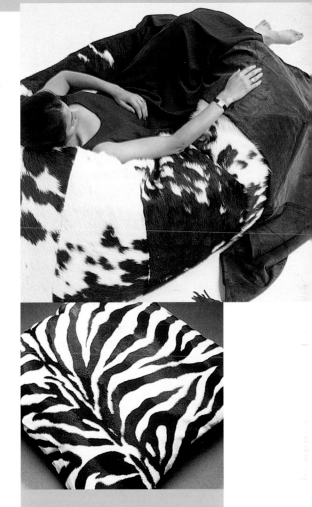

wildlife options
For a funkier look, try decorating a room with animal-print fabrics. The real thing is very durable, but avoid endangered species and skins obtained through cruelty!

fillings (made from foam rubber) are also germ resistant and washable, but they get hot in summer and can be sweaty.

Nylon was invented by the French manufacturer Dupont, along with Teflon and Lycra.

Originally it was used to replace silk in hosiery manufacture, but it is now used in a vast array of products. It is best used for outside furniture because it is water repellent and extremely strong.

Another new synthetic fiber that is very eco-friendly is Tencel. Like viscose, this is derived from wood pulp but does not use a chemical solvent. The resulting cloth, when mixed with cotton, is very strong, soft and colorfast.

NATURAL FILLINGS

No matter the quality of your fabric choice, it is the type and quality of the fillings that make or break upholstery and bedding.

ECO-TIP

Choosing the right fabric
Fabrics produced in an environmentally friendly way include organic cotton, sheep's wool, hemp yarn and Tencel, a man-made fabric derived from wood pulp. Choose fabrics in their natural colors, then dye them with natural dyes. Cushions with removable covers make them easy to wash, and dark-colored fabrics are best for sofas and chairs because they don't show the dirt as much as light-colored ones.

Down is the most expensive filling but it always plumps itself up and never loses its springiness. Down from the eider duck is the warmest and much of it is collected during the moulting season rather than from the slaughterhouse, making it an ethical and ecological filling. Use down in pillows and duvets for extra comfort.

Duck and goose feathers are not as warm, soft or springy as down, and you'll need nearly three times as many for the equivalent cushion because they are very fine. They are, however, cheap and long lasting. Some people have allergic reactions to feathers, in which case synthetic fibers provide a healthy alternative.

SYNTHETIC FILLINGS

There is a very good selection of these. Both acrylic and polyester wadding are washable and hypoallergenic but also need to be tightly packed into a rigid fabric casing in order to avoid becoming lumpy. Foam chips and blocks are cheap but not comfortable or long lasting. They also need to be treated with flame-retardant chemicals to reduce the risk of catching fire. After several

years of wear, blocks do crumble and the resulting waste is neither biodegradable nor reusable. Latex foam is made from natural rubber and lasts longer than does synthetic foam. It is especially good for using inside sofa seat cushions, while the sofa backrest and back cushions are best filled with feathers and down.

< covers, curtains and throws

Fabrics are a cheap and easy way to decorate your home, so explore the options and aim to color coordinate.

CLOSE-UP: UPHOLSTERY

Whether covered in leather or fabric, upholstered furniture was traditionally designed with a solid wood chassis, covered with horsehair and tied together with hessian and flax—all natural materials and all designed to last a long time. Cheaper, modern alternatives, such as those made from MDF, synthetic covers, foam and staples, may look similar in the showroom but will often wear badly, provide poor support and be hard to fix when damaged. When buying new furniture ask for details on how the furniture has been constructed, what has been used for the fillings and how easy it is to clean and replace sections of fabric.

Rooms for living

Each room in your home provides you with a protected space that should last for many years, grow with you and allow you to express yourself. Practical, beautiful, adaptable, harmonious, easy to clean and easy to live in, rooms should also conserve resources and help to improve the quality of our environment, both locally and globally. The American architect Frank Lloyd Wright said that a home should be woven like a rug so that it is tough, comfortable, beautiful and consistent. As we move from one room to the next, patterns and materials should repeat and hold the whole together. In addition, we should try to do more with less, remembering an old Japanese proverb, "a home which keeps the rain out and has enough food to keep us from starving—this is sufficiency."

Chapter Four

Entrances, halls and stairs

F ew people consider corridors, staircases and the entranceway when assessing their home's eco-worthiness. Yet these secondary spaces are just as vital as the main rooms and, with some creative thought, hold a great deal of design potential.

THE ENTRANCEWAY

This transitional space is the way in and out of your home. It should have an inviting face, keep warm air in and cold air out, have enough space for waiting and unloading, and be a place to greet and say good-bye. In order to fulfill these activities, it needs to be designed in a seamless way.

Since the entranceway is the most trafficked area of your home, avoid laying carpet, because this wears easily. Instead, install a large and tough coir mat and use hard flooring, such as stone or concrete covered with linoleum. Consider using a ceramic tile or paneled finish on the lower section of the wall to protect it from the frequent

> welcome home

Beyond a solid front door, every home needs an entry where you can take off overcoats, store wet umbrellas, hang up hats, take off mucky shoes, drop your keys, put down mail and leave messages.

knocks caused by incoming bikes, strollers and other household deliveries.

Keep the hallway relatively light in color, to help your eyes adjust between the bright outside and the darker interior. Ideally, install a window by the front door so you can see visitors and have natural light. To create soft lighting, connect the light switch by the door to desk lamps rather than overhead fixtures.

CORRIDORS AND STAIRS

Often considered a waste of space, these thoroughfares can be made more productive by incorporating them into the living space. A single, large, multifunctional room in which to lounge, dine and entertain can stretch from the back to the front of your home. With windows on two sides, there will be an ever-changing play of natural light in this room, giving you the opportunity to vary its use.

Where corridors are needed for privacy or structural reasons, try to keep them as short as possible. Try to design them so they incorporate as much storage as possible. They should also have access to natural light, either from skylights above or from internal glazing between the corridor and adjacent living rooms.

< overview
In a two-story home, open-plan living can also accommodate an open staircase, adding a third dimension to your house.

∧ safety precautions
All staircases should have banisters or railings, and any coverings should be nonslip. If you have children, avoid stairwells or steps with a steep gradient.

To prevent hallways from becoming blank, faceless and lifeless routes, hang lots of pictures or photos of family and friends along their walls. In larger homes, corridors and stairs may form part of a protected route in case of fire. Therefore, before making any major changes to these areas of your home, always check with an architect or contractor, who will advise you of any possible problems.

Corridors and stairs get the most wear in your home and therefore need tough finishes that will last well. Hard flooring and tiled walls are easy to keep clean while light colors will widen and brighten narrow spaces.

To save energy in hallways, close heating vents there and use low-energy lighting with timer switches that turn off automatically after a minute or so.

stylish storage

A basket on the stairs (above) is one way to gather items and avoid running up and down constantly. Storage ideas for larger entrances include (right) extended coat rails, hooks, rolling carts and high-level or slim-line shelves.

< versatility

If a corridor is wide enough, you can use it as an extra study space. If you would have to squeeze past a desk, however, then you should place your study area elsewhere.

Living rooms and lounging

Today's living rooms work hard and need to change moods quickly, from relaxation to formality or from entertainment to work. Since so much of our time at home is spent here, we should put as much of ourselves into the space as possible.

LOCATION

The living room needs to occupy the most comfortable part of the home. It should be quiet and restful, have good views and enough space to house seating, informal eating, storage and idle loafing. Ideally, it should face the afternoon or evening sun, which may mean that the traditional "front room" is totally inappropriate. Close to the garden and the kitchen, the main living space may need to take over the rear kitchen or even move upstairs so that it overlooks the back garden with stairs leading directly outdoors. If this is not possible, then open up the front room to the back so that light and views spread across the full depth of the floor.

Living rooms also need to break outside when the weather is good. One ideal way of achieving this is by replacing an existing window with French doors that you can open in the summer. This will also bring more light into the room and increase the connection between the indoors and outdoors, even when the doors are closed.

Better still, you will gain some more space by building a conservatory between the back garden and the living room. This way you will be able to capture a small part of the natural world and let it infiltrate your home for much of the year.

Another way of increasing the strength of your living-room space is to open it up to upper floors. This can be achieved either by incorporating the staircase into the living room or by breaking out part of the upper floor to create a double-height space.

SUITABLE FLOORING

Living rooms need to be comfortable and relaxing, and lounging on the floor is just as

> **minimalism**

This living room is neither cluttered by furniture nor confused by color. Each item sits alone with enough space to breathe, yet the whole is unified.

> **material options**

The ultimate eco-living room is one filled with natural fabrics, including wooden floorboards, leather chairs, muslin blinds and paper lanterns.

> storage ideas

Wood tables and wicker consoles are easy and cheap to put together, and they are far less taxing ecologically than the more common glass and steel cabinets.

important as sitting on a comfortable chair. Wood floors are fine, provided there are plenty of rugs and cushions, since this allows your guests the option of relaxing at floor level as well. A concrete floor is cold in winter but very cooling in summer. Leveled and polished, it creates a crisp and modern interior.

Between these two extremes lie natural fibers, linoleum and rubber, all of which have their particular pros and cons. Sea grass and hessian are strong textures that can sometimes overpower rooms containing modern furniture. They are also not particularly hard wearing, so well-trodden circulation routes will wear before the rest. Linoleum tends to age relatively well as layers of wax and dirt slowly deepen the surface. Rubber, on the

ECO-TIP

Planning for the future
One of the principles of eco-living is to furnish your home with items that will stay with you for years. Constantly changing your décor to suit your furniture, or vice versa, is hard on the wallet as well as the environment. Living-room furniture should be selected especially carefully because, if well chosen, it should adapt to your changing needs, and move with you from one home to the next. Never rush into selecting furniture and fixtures, and be sure to refer to the ecological checklist in chapter 7. In this way, you will ensure that your purchases really do stand up to the test of time.

v everyone's favorite

The sofa is probably the most expensive and long-lasting item of furniture in the living room, so choose carefully. Consider comfort, removable covers for easy cleaning and fire-retardant material.

other hand, will require yearly cleaning and polishing if it is to maintain its like-new finish, so bear this in mind.

Rather than installing wall-to-wall carpets, consider using mats and rugs that can be aired and dusted outside and replaced individually. Tiles and slates are best used more sparingly, either at the base of an old fireplace or as a centerpiece to a living space. An unpolished slab sitting at the center of a warm living room appears strange, but it will provide an interesting base for a pile of magazines or a gnarled piece of wood.

SHELVING SOLUTIONS
Living rooms are full of books, music, games and your favorite

light options
Small table lamps provide pools of light that wash walls or favorite reading areas (right). Large floor-to-ceiling windows allow lots of natural light into the room (below).

< low-level lounging

Sometimes relaxing on the floor is just as important as sitting on a comfortable chair, so furnish your living room with lots of rugs, cushions and beanbags.

art, so you will need somewhere to store all of these items. To retain an architectural rigor you might prefer fixed shelving with even spacing between the shelves. However, if your aim is to pack in as many books as possible, then adjustable shelving with pegged uprights and brackets is a must.

THE CEILING

The living-room ceiling is as significant as the floor, and a poorly decorated ceiling will let the rest of the room down.

The usual plasterboard ceiling hides wiring and provides fire protection between floors. In its simple way, it is a neat solution but it does make moving light fixtures a hassle and it adds little to the character of the room. In old buildings it may be possible to expose the joists and bring a touch of age to an otherwise modern space. You may want to avoid the issue of ceiling lights altogether and use floor and table lamps instead. This will leave a flat plane of color above your head.

Choose a light color to increase the feeling of space; only consider a dark ceiling finish if your ceiling is very high or you have large windows.

FIREPLACES

For many of us, the traditional fireplace remains the true focal point of the living room, with its mantelpiece housing our most treasured possessions. While an open fire is inefficient and not particularly healthy, the alternative of a blank wall and radiator or heating vent is hardly inspirational.

Outside major cities, wood fires are still allowed, but they are banned from some urban settings to reduce city smog and pollution.

To reduce smoke levels in the countryside, use well-dried wood. You can also help to minimize environmental damage by burning fallen trees and wood thinnings.

To make a truly environmental fire, burn wood in a stove and wrap the flue and pipes in a thick brick or concrete wall so that the heat can be stored in the living room but spread through the rest of your home.

CLOSE-UP: THE DAYBED

While sofas make comfortable places for lounging, they are often one-note items of furniture that don't offer much flexibility. Also, they are usually constructed of a complex mix of foam, metal springs and cheap wood by-products that are hard to fix or recycle. An interesting alternative is the modern chaise longue, the daybed. This should consist of a solid wooden frame made from beech or oak. To complement its one armrest, it should also have lots of comfortable feather cushions.

Kitchens and cooking

Today's kitchen is no longer a utility but a festival, filled with different textures, colors and smells. It is your home's soul and hearth, and it provides you with food, warmth and comfort. Rather than hiding this vital room away, make the kitchen a significant space in your home.

ALLOCATION

If the layout of your home allows it, consider having a combined kitchen and dining area. In smaller homes, do without the formality of separate cooking and dining rooms and open up a galley kitchen to the living room instead.

If you are building your kitchen from scratch and have a choice, situate it beside the garden or balcony so that you have easy access to light. Do not make the kitchen the sole occupant of the outside wall, however, since living rooms also need light and views.

Organize the layout of the kitchen so that you can flow smoothly from storage to preparation to cooking with adequate space for each. By putting the sink and range on the same surface, there will be less chance of spilling hot water when moving pots and pans about. Make sure you give yourself enough work surface on either side of the sink and the range, and allow plenty of room for waste separation and disposal around the preparation zone.

Ideally, there should be just a few paces between the preparation area, oven and sink. Known as the kitchen triangle, this setup allows you to work quickly, easily and safely.

> room with a view

When planning your kitchen space, utilize natural daylight by situating work surfaces next to windows. This way, you won't be working in your own shadow and will always have a good view.

REMOVABLE KITCHENS

These are now becoming very popular and for good ecological reasons. First of all, they are made from more durable materials than the melamine-faced chipboard characterizing installed kitchens. Secondly, the various elements can be moved around a room or

> clean and tidy

If you prefer a more minimal look for your kitchen, consider flat-faced cabinets. These allow you to keep your kitchen jumble out of sight and also cut down on maintenance. Food also stores better if kept cool and in the dark.

keywords > efficient hygienic organized safe

The Shaker kitchen

The Shakers, a group of devout Christians, formed toward the end of the eighteenth century in England before moving to the United States. Apart from their combined skills in agriculture and forestry, the Shakers became renowned for their high-quality furniture that was simple, practical and durable. Shaker furniture is traditionally made from local woods such as American oak and hickory. To copy the Shaker style in your kitchen, think minimal. Keep only a few items of well-made furniture and decorate using plain or subdued colors. One popular Shaker habit is to hang chairs on hooks on the walls when they are not being used. This creates more space in the kitchen and also makes the floor easier to clean.

taken with you if you move. Finally, the combination of solid wood, removable stone or stainless steel allows you to mix and match modern appliances with the older ones.

STORAGE IDEAS

Bearing in mind that fresh food should be stored in cool, well-ventilated spaces shaded from the sun, make kitchen storage as pleasant as possible.

Avoid glass cabinets and containers (because food should be stored out of direct light) but remember that a row of colorful jars on a window shelf can be just as beneficial to your well-being as a well-ordered cabinet. Plan your shelving so that everything is

∨ hang and stack

Space is at a premium in a kitchen so take full advantage of every storage opportunity. Everyday items can hang on hooks attached to nearby walls and surfaces (below). Carousel shelves are good for less-often used items (middle), while ceramic canisters are good for storing basic ingredients (far right).

LIVING NATURALLY

Eating good food
Relearn the delights of food by practicing the following habits:

• Choose local and fresh produce that is grown naturally and seasonally, stored carefully and prepared simply.

• Keep frozen and processed foods to a minimum and opt for more traditional storage methods, such as curing and preserving, since these keep foods fresh without the need for energy-consuming freezers.

• When buying foreign produce, stick to dry goods that are shipped at relatively little cost; avoid the fresh stuff that requires air-freighting in cool boxes and leaves local farmers with less than a tenth of the consumer price.

• Avoid overpackaged goods, sticking to simple and easily recycled containers, such as bottles and paper, instead.

visible and within easy reach; make sure deeper pullout shelving is at a low level, while narrow adjustable shelves are high up.

SURFACES

Cooking is a messy business, so countertops, floors and walls should all be resistant to water, oil and odors. Terrazzo, polished concrete, ceramics, slate and stone are good choices for flooring, since they are unaffected by heat or food and are very easy to keep clean. If you are prone to dropping things, then softer cork, linoleum or rubber floors will help to limit damage. Wood is another possibility although it is less resistant to water damage in the long run. A thick parquet floor with good joints is far better than thin wood veneers.

> **back-splash tiles**
Ceramic tiles are perfect materials for use in the kitchen because they are waterproof, easy to clean and eco-friendly, as well as economical.

You need to be able to wipe these surfaces so avoid any delicate paintwork. Ceramic tiles add scale, color and individuality, while stainless-steel sheeting creates a cool modern finish that is long lasting and easy to clean with mild detergents and adds the illusion of space to smaller rooms. Stainless steel can also be recycled at the end of its useful life. On other walls, try using tough mineral paint, cork or wood paneling.

WASTE

The kitchen should be the front-line for controlling waste disposal, especially since so much of it is generated there. Keep a bin for compostable food and make sure you have enough space inside for

< working surfaces
There are plenty of work surfaces to choose from; aim for quality over cost. Granite is a good choice because, although it is expensive, it is impervious to all it encounters. To avoid backache, make sure your cabinets are built to a suitable height.

the separation of items that you can either reuse in the home, recycle, or dispose of completely. The basic categories that you need to allow for are compostable foodstuffs, paper and fabric, metals, glass, plastic, toxins and mixed waste. If you watch what goes into the garbage can and aim to avoid buying products with unnecessary packaging, you can reduce waste by at least half. For more information on eco-friendly waste disposal, see chapter 6.

GETTING THE LIGHT RIGHT
It is vital that the kitchen be lit in such a way that you can prepare

∧ **light and clean**
Maximize daylight by leaving windows unobscured, placing a table by the window and keeping kitchen surfaces light in color. This light limestone kitchen floor is eco-friendly and creates a stunning, yet simple ambience.

> ### ECO-TIP
>
> **Low-energy cooking**
> The best eco-cooking methods are either to heat ingredients quickly over high heat or to slowly stew them at a low temperature. Pressure cookers, microwave ovens, steamers and quick stir-frying all use a lot less energy than baking or boiling in open pans. When you do use the oven, get the most out of the heat by cooking in bulk. Better still, avoid using energy in the first place by making lots of salads and eating seasonal fruits.

food hygienically and safely. Maximize daylight by having a table next to the window and making sure that the window is unobscured by furniture or tall plants. Choosing kitchen surfaces in a pale color will further help to reflect daylight.

As for electric lighting, small linear fluorescent tubes are an excellent and efficient source of lighting for food preparation and cooking areas. You can also use them inside glass cabinets to show off your favorite china.

ENERGY-SAVING MEASURES
Simple technological innovations, such as level marks on your kettle or the timer on your oven, go a long way in preventing you from

Despite the homey qualities associated with Agas, these stoves are relatively expensive to run, so they are really only suitable for very large families who have a continuous demand for hot food and water. Urban dwellers should stick to gas stoves, which use less fuel than electric ones and switch on and off at the turn of a dial. They should also be cool to touch, so choose ovens with good wall insulation.

Ventilation

Because gas stoves produce fumes and cooking food produces steam and odors, it's important to install a ventilation system in the kitchen that draws out air when you are cooking. Recirculating range hoods do not solve the problem and only remove some of the grease and steam.

Ideally you should install an extractor hood connected to a heat exchange unit, so that the heat from cooking can be captured and returned to the house while moist air is channeled outdoors (see also page 40). If this is not possible, then make sure the fan runs only when it is absolutely needed.

∧ effective lighting

Low-voltage downlights illuminate kitchen work surfaces and countertops. They need to be carefully sited to avoid creating shadows when you work. Installing a dimmer switch will allow you to change the atmosphere from a practical working space to a more intimate eating area.

using energy in a wasteful manner, so try to fit out your kitchen with these items. Avoid filling the kettle with more water than you need, and try not to rely too much on electrical gadgets such as beaters when manual ones will work just as well. Using a pressure cooker or microwave oven will also reduce the amount of energy you use to cook.

The optimum stove

For people who live in a rural area, wood-burning stoves like those made by Aga provide a renewable source of power both for cooking and for heating. The classic kitchen stove is being continually updated with modern versions able to run cleanly with low wood consumption and supply heat to the home.

> economy measures

When choosing kitchen equipment for your eco-friendly home, always consider energy efficiency over style. Take advantage of technological advances by buying a combined fridge-freezer (top), a range with an air-cleansing hood (middle) and a microwave oven (bottom).

A low-energy alternative is to use passive stack vents to draw the warm air from the room naturally, but this can only be done if you have direct access to the roof.

The fridge-freezer
A high-efficiency combination fridge-freezer will use relatively little power but still have room for all your basic needs. To keep it running at its best, defrost it every six months and keep it well organized. Try not to freeze too much food, keep your fridge-freezer as compact as possible and never put warm items in the fridge.

CLOSE-UP: POTS AND PANS

You should only ever need to buy one set of pots and pans, so carefully consider the materials and the craftsmanship involved in making them. Stainless steel is a hard-wearing material but pots need to have an aluminum or copper base for good heat conduction and retention. Aluminum pans share the same qualities as stainless steel, but some say they affect the taste of certain foods. All pots and pans should have straight sides that are fairly deep. Their lids should fit snugly and the handle should be sturdy, welded to the pan and have a hole from which to hang when storing. Classic enameled cast-iron pots can last a century and are always worth the investment.

Dining rooms and eating

For a family, sitting down together for an evening meal and catching up on the day's events should be one of the most important times of the day. A separate dining area not too far away from the kitchen is the ideal place for this. With some fancy place settings and additional décor, this room can take on a more formal air and be used to entertain friends and colleagues.

MULTIFUNCTIONAL

The traditional dining table sits in its own room, surrounded by ten chairs, used only for formal meals. This can be a waste of space and precious resources, so aim to use your dining room more often, perhaps as a work area or where your kids can do their homework. Better yet, choose folding, sliding and removable surfaces. Tables in their simple form are legs and tops, and if you buy separate components that fit together you will be able to take off the table top and lean it against the wall, creating extra floor space on which children can play or guests can stay over.

THE DINING TABLE

In addition to comfort, surface and shape should be your primary considerations when choosing a dining table. Those that are round and oval make conversation easier and have no sharp or awkward

< dress up or down
A cheap and easy way to change the atmosphere of your dining room to suit the occasion is with fabric chair coverings and tablecloths.

∧ **dual purpose**
If space is at a premium in your home, use your dining room as a work area. A large dining table is also an ideal place for kids to sit down and do their homework together.

< **close to the source**
A partition with backlighting creates the illusion of a separate dining area, while still having the convenience of being close to the kitchen.

corners. However, square and rectangular tables are easier to move against the wall when you want to use the room for another purpose. Consider a table with drop leaves for ultimate adaptability. Hard materials, such as marble, glass and slate, are easy to maintain, although wood is the most comforting surface. As for table linen, choose fabric cloths and napkins to soften nonwooden surfaces and use hard place mats and paper napkins to create the opposite effect.

Suitable materials
When choosing a dining table, remember that it will be used frequently and, no matter how careful you are, will still suffer from food spills and damage from sharp or hot implements. Wood is

v wood, glorious wood
Sustainable wood in all its forms is light, long lasting and easy to clean, so it is the ideal material for dining furniture. Chairs should be comfortable, so if they don't have upholstery, attach a cushion to their seats.

two of a kind
Nothing beats fine bone china as the ultimate long-lasting, classically attractive material for dinnerware (above right). However, you might like to purchase some cheap and cheerful items for everyday use (above left).

may be a better choice if you have young children, but whatever material you choose, they should all give firm support for the back and spine.

FLOORING

The best flooring materials for the dining room are those that are hard wearing and easy to sweep or wipe clean. Stripped or polished floorboards and linoleum or cork tiles are all good choices. Because food gets dropped, drinks get spilled and candles leak melted wax, carpet is not a good idea. If wall-to-wall carpeting is already in place, position your table on a rug over the carpet. If you have children, consider putting a sheet of plastic under the table to catch all the crumbs and keep your floor clean.

the ideal choice for a dining table. Veneer-coated tables will become damaged quickly, so protect them by placing a felt underlay and tablecloth on top. Solid oak, beech and even softwoods like pine are excellent woods for tables, provided they are protected with hard wax oils.

While cheaper melamine over plywood is less attractive, you can always cover it with a favorite tablecloth, which hides the less-than-perfect top.

DINING CHAIRS

Chairs should complement both the table and the room itself. Stacking chairs are good because they save space and can add interest to the walls if hung up. Director's chairs are multipurpose and you can usually buy extra seats and backs in different colors.

This not only prolongs their useable life but is also an easy way to change your décor. Upholstered chairs in natural fibers are now commonplace and are the most comfortable form of seating. Coverings can even be treated to protect them from stains. Solid wood or metal chairs

< cloth versus paper
Good-quality linen napkins will last a lifetime and are much more eco-friendly than disposable ones. Placing them in silver napkin holders will also bring a touch of class to the table.

Bedrooms and sleeping

This is the simplest room to decorate because it really only has a few purposes: to help you sleep, dream, make love and wake up refreshed. A generous and comfortable bed is the key to achieving these but, unfortunately, we seem to fill the bedroom with other distractions that merely add to the clutter in our lives. Making the bedroom a storage space, a dressing room, a makeup parlor or an extra study can lead to complicated solutions.

LOCATION AND LAYOUT

Bedrooms demand privacy, peace and a little natural light. Ideally, choose a room that catches the early-morning sun, away from noise and pollution. Since it is very much a nighttime room, alternative locations toward the north of your home will also work, whereas south-facing bedrooms receive valuable sunshine that would better benefit daytime activities. In warm climates, the bedroom should definitely be kept shady and cool, with good access to natural breezes.

For privacy, separate the children's rooms from the parents', perhaps using the bathroom as an intermediate room. The French architect Le Corbusier went one step further and, in his Unité d'Habitation, placed the parents' bedrooms at one end of the flat, close to the living room, with the kids' bedroom at the opposite end.

Bedrooms on the ground floor of your home may seem strange but don't be afraid of considering this more radical approach. If the windows are sheltered from direct view, they may actually be more suited to this floor because it is generally cooler at night and there is more privacy.

THE BED

In Asia, the bed is often little more than a thickening of the floor matting; a traditional futon laid directly on the bedroom floor is a neat and simple solution for a restful night. During the day it can be rolled up and away or taken outside to air when needed.

The downside of a futon is that it doesn't give you a comfortable

differing needs

The bed you choose for your children will obviously be different from your own, but both should be easy to dismantle for portability and optimum flexibility.

space for an evening read or breakfast in bed and that's where the Western headboard and frame come into their own. Beds that don't lie low to the ground also have the benefit of providing storage space out of view.

Bed frames and supports

These come in many shapes and sizes, the standard being the fabric-covered box spring, which is neither attractive nor long lasting.

The better alternative is to buy simple slatted wood frames that you can varnish with linseed-based oils to match your décor.

Mattresses

While futons are made from simple cotton wadding, Western mattresses are constructed from metal springs and synthetic foams. Obviously, the more you pay the more you will get in return and an expensive mattress lasts longer and provides more support for your back than a cheaper one does. That said, a firm futon that is properly cared for offers all the support that you need.

SUITABLE SURFACES

The bedroom floor is perhaps the one place in your home where a more luxurious floor finish will

∧ occasional beds

Futons are ideal for storing away until you have a guest. Not only do futons take up far less space than Western mattresses, but they can also be used as a sofa when placed on a fold-up base.

add to your comfort and be relatively easy to maintain.

A wood floor will provide a clean surface, and the addition of a thick rug at the base of your bed or to its side will give your feet a comfortable and warm landing. In comparison, a stone floor might simply shock you into action. If you have a no-shoes policy, then you may want to install a wool carpet, although the fact that most of it will sit under the bed or other furniture makes its usefulness debatable. Alternatively, you may prefer the rough texture of natural fibers, such as coir matting. The key is choosing a floor that is easy to keep dust free. This way, the air in your bedroom encourages ease and rest, rather than antagonizing your lungs.

LIGHTING

In the bedroom, lighting should be relatively subdued and close at hand. Bedside and table lamps are far better options than overhead fixtures. Directional task lamps can either point toward the wall for a gentle wash of light or provide excellent directed light for late-night reading without disturbing your sleeping partner. Lighting is also useful at the dressing table and by wardrobes.

keep it neat

Ideal bedroom storage should be built in, making it a part of the room's repertoire. Cleverly concealed cabinets made from ash wood can even double up as an extended headboard (right). If you choose free-standing pieces of furniture, make sure they are made from natural, eco-friendly materials (above).

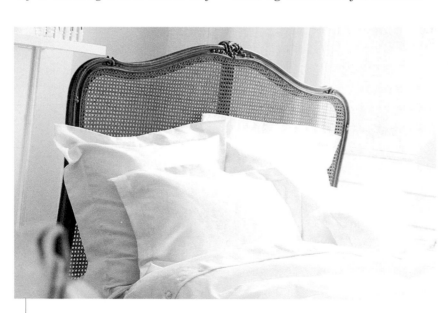

Eternally yours: the headboard

In the past, the ornately carved marital headboard was a fitting part of the new family's dowry and was treasured from youth to old age before being handed down to the next generation. If the idea of sleeping in your parents' or grandparents' bed is a little disconcerting, seek out an old-fashioned bed frame or headboard in your local antique store.

If you are a heavy sleeper, choose some lightweight curtains that will allow the morning light to filter through. Light sleepers will require thicker, lined curtains to enable sleeping in on the weekends.

DECORATION IDEAS

Many bedrooms today have either a virginal or sensual air. Some people prefer a rich tapestry of

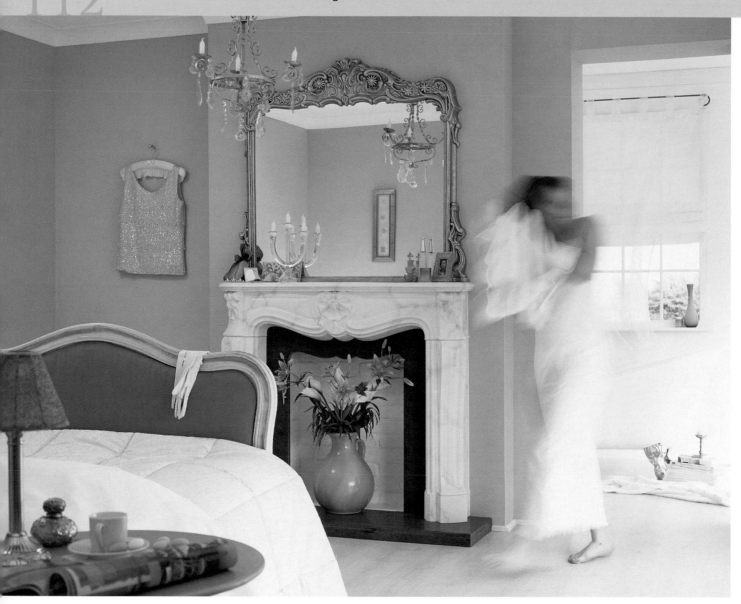

exotic art, while others treat the bedroom as a clean, almost monastic cell.

Although there are fewer ecological considerations in the bedroom than in the other rooms of your home, the following thoughts will give you an idea of how you might go about decorating.

The sensuous bedroom will have rich and deep colors that create an enclosure around your bed, with subdued lighting. Conversely, a white bedroom with pale wood and light fabrics will need little artificial lighting during the day and will help you to rise with the sun. However, it may seem too clinical at night, particularly when the moon shining through curtains casts an eerie light.

Decorating the ceiling

Perhaps our lasting memories of the childhood bedroom are of small fluorescent stars twinkling in the darkened sky on the ceiling as we slowly drifted off to slumber land.

While this imagery seems overblown to most adults, it does serve to remind us that the ceiling is an important design element in the bedroom. Where they might go unnoticed in other rooms of your home, poor-quality light fixtures and badly finished wallpaper will remain an eyesore in the bedroom. While a simply painted ceiling

< **the feminine touch**
A crystal chandelier and a restored rococo mirror placed on a soft lilac background create a feeling of understated opulence.

might be all that's needed, consider alternative ceiling finishes, such as tongue-and-groove wood paneling, since these add character to your nightly view.

Window effects
The bedroom window itself may be the perfect space to start decorating your eco-bedroom.

A light-colored sill and frame make a perfect place to let the morning pour into the room. If it is deep enough, the sill could also provide a platform for plants, a cushion and a pile of books for your morning read.

The end of a window alcove provides a neat space for a set of thick curtains that will keep the heat in at night. Alternatively you might set a bed platform itself at sill height so that you can wake to an immediate view of the outside world, with cooling air close at hand on a sultry summer night.

LINEN
This should be easy to clean and long lasting. Avoid synthetic sheets and blankets because they

∧ **early-morning call**
Using an old-fashioned wind-up alarm clock is a way to avoid electromagnetic radiation and unnecessary use of electricity in the bedroom.

attract dust and don't allow your skin to breathe properly. Duck-down duvets are a practical and easy-care alternative, although feather fills are allergenic to some (see pages 82–83).

Polyester or acrylic duvet fillings are available at a lower cost and can last for an equally long time. Always store duvets that are made with feather fillings and natural fiber bed linen in warm and dry conditions so they are safe from moths and damp air.

Mattress pads are also advisable because they will keep the mattress cleaner for longer and will provide extra warmth and softness.

< **fresh and fancy**
Linen is the ideal fabric for bedding because not only is it a long-lasting, eco-friendly material, but it is also cool against the skin in summer.

Bathrooms and bathing

Although a necessity, washing is the one time and place in the day where we can contemplate our navels in peace, away from the frenzy of modern living. In many homes, the bathroom is hidden away and filled with pastel fiberglass and plastics, vinyl flooring, bare and washed-out tungsten bulbs and a whirring fan: practical, but hardly natural, inspiring or long lasting. But times are changing and we are beginning to relearn the gentle art of bathing, taking what was functional and hidden out of the closet and talking happily about hygiene, sewage and efficiency.

LOCATION

In most homes a bathroom's location is fixed by the existing plumbing. Unless you can clearly see a better way of arranging your home, you will most likely have to make the most of things with this limitation. If you can relocate your plumbing, try moving the bathroom to an outer wall, since the resulting natural light and

> bathing in grandeur
If you have enough space in your bathroom, install a freestanding bathtub and take the art of bathing to a higher level. Freestanding tubs also provide a focal point in large bathrooms.

ventilation help to create a more relaxing environment. Also, modifications to plumbing are easier to make when there is access to an outside wall. If there is space under the stairs or at the end of a corridor, consider building a separate room for the toilet. Not only is this convenient, but it creates more room for a bathing space and it is also healthier to separate the two very different basic functions.

Try to avoid having more than one bathroom per home, since multiple bathrooms use more space, more material and generally lead to more use (or waste). If you do need more bathing space, create a shower room instead.

BATHROOM FURNITURE
The furniture that we choose for our bathrooms lasts longer than that in any other room in our home, so ensuring that they are both beautiful and efficient is vitally important. Collectively, the

> internal warmth
Surrounded by other centrally heated rooms in your home, the bathroom is usually quite easy to heat and keep warm. Heated towel racks also encourage warmth; if your bathroom doesn't have a window, view this positively because it will also help to keep heat in.

keywords > energy conserving fresh hygienic

bath, toilet, shower and sink use three-quarters of the entire water supply for your home and the energy used to heat water might make up half your total gas or electricity bills. It's especially important, therefore, to be mindful of water and energy conservation methods when choosing these items.

Decide whether freestanding or built-in equipment suits your bathroom best. A freestanding tub and shower provide a focal point to larger bathrooms, while a built-in bathtub tiled into the wall and floor will provide the best use of space in a smaller one.

BATHS AND SHOWERS

In Roman times, daily bathing was a public and shared experience, from the changing rooms to a hot scrub bath (the *caldarium*), to the bustling and noise-filled warm pool (the *tepidarium*) and then to a final plunge into the cold *frigidarium*. The public baths were considered a sign of civilization and often one of the first buildings to be built after the Romans vanquished a neighboring barbarian town. Private baths were rare and even emperors used to make occasional visits to the public pools.

bathing space

In smaller bathrooms, a shower over the tub provides you with two bathing options (above). If you have more space available, then you can even consider installing a bidet for added hygiene (left).

stepping out

A bamboo bath mat (top) is water resistant and more durable than other materials. If you prefer a softer landing, however, use a cotton bath mat (above).

< salvage solutions

Architectural reclamation yards are great sources for old tubs. If you find a copper tub, make sure it's small, because copper is a conductor of heat, so your water will cool quickly.

But Roman cleanliness was particular to the time and place. By the Middle Ages, bathing was considered dangerous because it was thought to upset the thermal equilibrium of the body. Instead, people used perfumes to hide body odor. It was only in the eighteenth century, when doctors began to

∧ **bathroom tidy**
To have your bathing accessories within reach, choose a shower hanger with a durable and tarnish-resistant finish.

∧ **shower safety**
Shower trays come in several shapes and sizes, which means you can install a shower cubicle in almost any corner of your bathroom. Make sure the cubicle is installed with a well-sealed door that prevents water from splashing onto the floor outside. Specially sealed spotlights are also available for showers. Always cover shower walls with water-resistant tiles.

recognize the importance of clean air and clean water, that a daily wash became fashionable again. And it wasn't until the nineteenth century and the arrival of cholera from the East that the first municipally supplied fresh water and fast-flowing sewers allowed us the enjoyment of taking a bath every day. Even today, a daily tub of warm water is a luxury in most parts of the world.

Hygienically and ecologically, showers beat baths hands down. They flush away the day's dirt or the night's sleep more rapidly than a dip in a bath, using less water and less energy than a bath. Yet nothing compares to a good, long soak in the comfort and privacy of your own bathtub. Use your own judgment to achieve a balance between comfort, hygiene and care for resources.

The ideal shower is one that uses minimal water but provides an invigorating wash. Avoid the modern "power showers" available in Britain because these can use even more water than a conventional bath. Instead, opt for specially adapted shower heads that aerate the water but restrict the total volume. Avoid electrically heated water systems, because these use two to three times as much energy as gas-fueled water heaters.

Plastic bathtubs don't require a lot of energy for their manufacture, but they scratch easily and will look worn and old quickly. If you

classic colors
White fixtures (top) offer the maximum flexibility, whereas a colored suite is likely to lose its visual appeal over time and therefore is more likely to be replaced. Alternatively, opt for a clean, modern metal look (above).

can, look for smaller and deeper traditional cast-iron baths. Many of these have been replaced by fiberglass or plastic bathtubs, which are fairly harmless ecologically but are neither as beautiful nor as long lasting as their cast-iron or pressed-steel equivalents. If you have an old cast-iron bath with scratches, instead of replacing it, get it re-enameled and save yourself some money and the scrap heap some waste.

Toilets
In the eighteenth century, long before the flush toilet was invented, defecation was a relatively public affair and we used to chat away to friends while perched on the *chaise percee* under which was hidden the chamber pot. In the nineteenth century this gave way to the privy. The toilet bowl transcended mere utilitarian concerns and became an object of private comfort, fitted out with magazine racks, cast with ornamental designs and culminating in a design by the unfortunately named Thomas Crapper. To this day, the world is still divided between those who use the toilet as a small-scale private library and those who want to get it all over with as quickly and effectively as possible.

Many homes are still fitted with older toilets that use more than 3 gallons of water each flush. With a little effort, this can be reduced by a quarter, simply by putting a couple of bricks in the tank. Better still, replace an older toilet with a dual-flush model that allows you to decide whether you need a 1-gallon or a 3-gallon flush. The toilet bowls are specially shaped so that they remove waste efficiently with minimum water.

At the most ecological end of the market are composting toilets. These use no water and create perfectly good compost for your garden. Although they cost more than the savings you'll make from reduced water use, they do make economic sense in dry regions and in situations when you are aiming to be completely self-sufficient.

Most commercial toilet paper is made from bleached paper in a high-energy process. Non-bleached recycled papers may be less luxurious, but they are cheaper, often decompose more quickly and are just as effective. They are a must if you are considering treating sewage waste in the garden.

Sinks
These are generally available in porcelain or stainless steel, both of

basin basics
v Kitchen-sized sinks are a popular choice in many modern bathrooms, but they require huge quantities of water to fill. It is much easier to wash your face in a shallow sink, and you'll waste less water too.

∧ au naturel
Not only does a wet shave give a much better result than an electric shaver, it is also a much better eco-choice. This is because you don't need to use electricity. Always avoid plastic disposable razors.

they gather dust easily. Ceramic or glass dishes are good for holding soap and if you buy attractive or textured types they will be beautiful objects in themselves.

Spare towels and laundry can be kept in a louvered cabinet, which will help to keep the bathroom tidy. If you have a water heater in your bathroom, consider building a cabinet around it—it is great for drying and airing clothes and towels you have just washed. As for drying wet towels, a simple hydronic towel warmer connected to the hot water supply will serve this purpose while keeping your bathroom warm at the same time. In the absence of a heated towel rack, keep the towels you are using on a valet or drying rack, which allow you to spread them

which are long lasting and environmentally responsible materials. See if you can get them fitted with spray taps that reduce the amount of water you use by aerating the water through fine nozzles. The resulting spray is just as effective at wetting and cleaning your skin, but it halves the amount of water you use. Existing taps can be modified with simple (although, it has to be said, not very attractive) adaptors, or you can buy well-designed new taps if you are upgrading your bathroom. Always use a stopper rather than running water straight down the drain when washing your face or hands.

Keep your medicines and toiletries in a lockable cabinet above the sink. Open shelves are not a good idea place to store makeup and medicine because

CLOSE-UP: BATH SOAPS

Natural soaps and cleansing oils will help to add color to the bathroom and are also more friendly, both for you and the environment. There are now many soaps made with vegetable bases such as palm, coconut and jojoba oils. Translucent glycerine soaps are less alkaline than ordinary soaps and also have an attractive look. Milk and honey soaps are good for sensitive skin. Other effective bath additives include epsom salts, which help to relax muscles and joints; aromatherapy oils; and herbs. Similarly, oatmeal or bran can be tied in a square of muslin and hung from the hot tap so hot water is allowed to run through. Both grains have a soothing effect on the skin.

out evenly to dry. Towels and robes don't tend to dry very well on a peg on the back of the door and could also contribute to creating a somewhat musty, moldy atmosphere in the bathroom.

Cleaning fluids should be kept separately from toiletries so store these and other less attractive bathroom necessities in low-level cabinets under the sink or under raised decks next to the bath and shower area.

BATHROOM SURFACES

If they are to last a long time and remain beautiful, bathroom floors and walls need to be watertight, slip resistant and able to cope with heat and moisture.

Good flooring options for the bathroom include cork, linoleum, terrazzo or local slate. Avoid carpets, natural fiber or wood because these are all prone to water damage, harbor mold and require frequent replacement.

Ceramic tiles provide a beautiful, reliable and long-lasting finish and can handle any volume of water without damage. They can also be thoroughly washed to help maintain a clean and healthy environment. If tiling a whole wall proves too expensive, confine it to backsplashes around the bath and sink, and use external-quality plaster, either bare or with a tint of natural color added to the mix, for the rest of the wall.

WINDOWS

Where possible, a bathroom should have a window to allow

∧ take your pick

There is a huge array of materials with which to decorate your bathroom walls and floors. Depending on the colors, textures and patterns you choose, these can help you transform a functional utility space into a stylish and relaxing room. Suitable bathroom materials include (clockwise from top left) rubber tiles, old vinyl floor tiles that are revitalized with special paints, ceramic tiles and stone tiles.

in natural light and ventilation. The sunlight can be diffused through a linen blind for privacy or through forest friendly plants and shrubs placed on the window sill for a tropical feel. If your window has a private view, let the stars shine in at night. In cooler climates, use low-e double-glazing (see page 38), because this reduces both heat

loss and condensation that forms on cold surfaces.

Protect wooden window frames and sills from warping by using water-resistant wax or water-resistant natural paints. Tiled sills and surroundings are easier to maintain because they are more water resistant, and light-colored tiles are even better because they reflect daylight into the room.

Slotted brickwork (bricks laid with open holes for windows) and wood louvres are good window options because they allow adequate levels of ventilation and light to filter through, and they also connect your bathroom to the outdoors. If you do choose this option use wire mesh to keep insects and other troublemakers on the right side of the window.

LIGHTING

While natural light can provide just the bathroom atmosphere you want, you'll need to consider nighttime lighting too. Perhaps the lowest-energy lighting is

lighting and atmosphere

Combined with your favorite incense, candlelight provides a soothing background glow while you bathe (left). If you can, place your bathroom in a location facing the rising sun (below). This way, you will be able to soak up the early-morning sunshine as you luxuriate in the water.

candlelight. Other low-energy lights for bathrooms include compact fluorescent bulbs, miniature fluorescent tubes and halogen spot lights (see pages 25–28). Lighting levels can be low throughout the bathroom, but with a more intense light source near the bathroom mirror for makeup, shaving and checking out the medicine cabinet.

VENTILATION

It is especially important that the bathroom be well ventilated since moist air and surfaces easily become traps for bacteria and mold. Ventilation is also paramount in keeping this room fresh and clean. An electrically operated bathroom fan, the natural chimney effect of a passive stack vent and simply an open window are the best ways to achieve good ventilation.

Bathroom fans

Although these run on electricity, only a small amount of energy is

consumed in return for a good level of ventilation. By connecting fans to a light switch or using a humidity controller, the fan will run only when it is really needed, limiting its energy use even further. The first rule for installing a fan in the bathroom is to make sure it is a quiet one, since nothing is more inhibiting to relaxation than the incessant drone of a noisy fan. The second consideration is to ensure that the fan is neither too big nor too small for the job.

You can also buy bathroom fans with air-to-air heat exchangers, which recover the energy in the exhaust air (see page 40). These units are provided with two fans, one to push air into the room and one to draw air out. The cold outside air is drawn through a series of metal plates that are warmed by the exhaust air, recovering about 60 percent of the heat. They are good energy savers in cold climates, but not really necessary if you keep the bathroom cool.

Passive stack vents

These act like miniature chimneys in your bathroom and should also be fitted with light and humidity controllers to avoid throwing away

warm house air. The chimney is made from a small plastic pipe with a vent outlet in the roof. When the passive stack vent is open, any wind passing over the roof helps to draw warm air out of the bathroom. These vents can be used only if your bathroom has easy access to a roof, and they are most successful when installed at the top of a pitched roof.

< made to last
The thick pile that constitutes traditional bath towels also makes them prone to mildew and bacteria because they are hard to dry. The alternative waffle towel is ultra absorbent, but also quick drying.

ECO-TIP

Greenhouse in your bathroom
The humid atmosphere of the bathroom suits many water-loving plants, especially if there is natural light. You can also make a miniature green house to germinate bulbs year-round by boxing in a window sill with secondary glazing. Useful plants for a window box include herbs, salads, strawberries and small tomatoes. Even internal bathrooms can be productive spaces. You can even grow mushrooms under the bathroom sink! If you don't feel like maintaining plants for food in your bathroom, ferns and other forest-friendly plants love a cool, dark and moist room.

Studies and home working

Working from home can be the best or the worst of both worlds. For some, it means giving up the daily commute and being able to spend more time with the family. For others, it can seem like a jail sentence, being stuck between the same four walls, unable to share ideas, meet new people or discover the rest of the world.

Successful home-working usually happens when you make a conscious effort to separate work from the other aspects of your home life. There is nothing worse than waking up to see a computer terminal staring unblinking from the dressing table or to find paints and other art materials scattered around the kitchen. If you work from home, it is a good idea to have some sort of transitional process, be it mental or physical, to distinguish between relaxing in your home and working in your home. Strolling to the typewriter in the shed at the far side of the garden or climbing up the last flight of stairs to the attic are some

> classic bureaux
If you don't need a large work surface, consider a well-made wooden bureau. You might even be able to use the wooden desk you had as a child, which will give your office a more homey feel.

examples of this. You should also hang a sign on your door, which indicates that you are working and are not to be disturbed.

SPACE REQUIREMENTS
The space you need will naturally depend on what it is you do, but the general rule of thumb is that you'll need between 25 and 30 square feet of space. It is unlikely that you can give up very much of your home to this one activity, but where possible, try to make your office in a room that is separate from your general home life; a study or spare bedroom is ideal. The space needs to have good natural light and ventilation, which means having a window surface that is between 20 and 40 percent of the floor area. Any less than this and the room will need artificial light for longer; any greater and it will overheat in the summer and require more heating in the winter.

SUITABLE DIRECTIONS
Art, writing and computer work are often best done in a north-facing room where the even light is kinder to the eyes. That said, a south-facing room is also fine if it has good adjustable external shading; an east-facing room will have gentle light in the afternoon

unusual corners

If you don't have the luxury of dedicating a whole room to your study, you can still create office space using some careful planning. For rooms with high ceilings, an effective solution is to build a mezzanine (left), which will double the wall and floor space available to you and bring you closer to the light. Alternatively, convert the space under the stairs (below).

when the sun has moved away. Avoid rooms that are affected by the noise and pollution of passing traffic. A room with a pleasant view is preferable to one without.

Remember that work is far less stressful when everything has a

> **office accessories**
A good desk lamp (right) is essential if you want to prevent eyestrain. Choose one that pivots for maximum flexibility. A diary bound in natural leather (center) makes a classier alternative to electronic organizers, and a good fountain pen (bottom) is not only a joy to use but also more ecological than disposable ballpoints.

ECO-TIP

Efficient home working
Use a portable computer that consumes little space or energy, produces far less screen radiation and is easier to move around than a bulky desktop machine. If you use a desktop computer, make sure it's Energy Star compatible. Avoid using screen savers because, despite the name, they actually waste energy since the monitor is still on. Always aim to have multipurpose equipment rather than lots of small items. Today, a single piece of equipment can act as a fax, telephone, printer and photocopier, and it will use less space, energy and materials than the individual items combined. It often costs less as well. E-mail will reduce the amount of paper you use, which should always be recycled. When you print, use both sides, and reuse single-sided paper. When you do visit clients or colleagues, use your bike or public transportation instead of the car.

place, so give yourself plenty of horizontal room both for laying out work and for storing work materials. When it comes to choosing desk accessories and storage systems, avoid the clinical look of most plastic or metal items and choose simple plywood boxes and holders that are gentler on the eye and the planet. Recycled cardboard magazine holders are fine for organizing information, and open wooden shelving on adjustable brackets will help you to store your files and accounts.

YOUR DESK AND LIGHTING
Obviously, the size of the desk you require will depend on the type of work you do, but it should always be long lasting and attractive.

The best position for your desk is next to an outside wall and at right angles to the window. This way, your eyes don't suffer from glare when you look up from your work. This will also make it far easier to open the window or close the blinds when the weather changes. Use a task lamp directly over your work area so that you can see clearly on overcast days.

Adjustable desk lamps that have fluorescent or low-voltage halogen bulbs provide the most flexibility.

COMFORT AND QUALITY

Whatever work you do and however you do it, always make sure that you are working comfortably. If your work involves using a computer, make sure the monitor is at eye level to reduce neck strain. If you are doing manual work, set the bench height so that you don't have to bend over. Have an alternative place to work that allows you to stand and work at the same time, such as a high, tilted drafting table with a flat adjacent surface. Choose a chair that is adjustable and supports your lower back.

The overall atmosphere of your work environment is also important. Surround yourself with fond memories that will cheer you up through duller days, such as pictures of your family and friends or simple objects of nature. Fill the room with plants and water them when you're lost for words. As soon as cabin fever strikes, get away from your desk.

Just as in the rest of your home, avoid toxic materials and energy-consuming appliances. Buy a nice, textured rug to add some color to the room. Take your shoes off and stretch your toes: make the most of being your own office manager.

v easy-access files

Home-working tends to generate a lot of paperwork, so you will need plenty of shelving to store invoices and records of accounts. Choose files made from recycled cardboard and try to reuse them whenever possible.

Studios

As we become richer, we are often filled with an incessant desire to own bigger and better things. Living small demands an alternative vision. Size does matter, but sometimes the smaller something is, the better it can be. The key is to look for quality over quantity, things that last rather than things that shout.

GOOD PLANNING

One of the benefits of living small is that it is far easier to make the space your own, but you do need to be well organized so there is space for work, entertaining, sleep and relaxation. In nature, different plants and animals use the same space at different times of the day, and this "stacking" is the key to making a success of small spaces.

Ceiling height

If you have the option, an extra foot or two of ceiling height is more valuable than a few extra square feet of floor space. A taller but small room will not only seem

> compact and bijou

In a small kitchen, maximizing the work surfaces is particularly important. This can be achieved by mounting microwaves and other kitchen appliances on the wall.

larger, it will also be brighter and capable of accommodating raised platforms, which add to the illusion of space. You can even locate the kitchen and shower room under a raised bed and storage platform or create level changes that provide additional storage space underneath them. A 3-foot-wide platform a couple of feet above the floor will give you the feeling of entering a different space and also provide you with loads of low-level storage underneath.

Clever plumbing

To minimize the space taken up by plumbing, make sure you locate your utility areas next to each other so that you can share items rather than having duplicates. One large sink might well be enough for washing your face, your dishes and your clothes.

Illusions of grandeur

Light-colored walls and floors create an illusion of space and spread daylight deeper into your home, which means you can use lower-wattage bulbs without straining your eyes. Having lots of windows and greenery will also increase the sense of space in a small home. Ideally, windows should reach down to the floor, and floor surfaces inside and out should reflect plants on either side of the glazing.

APPROPRIATE FURNITURE

Choose small furniture that is modular or mobile, folds up or rolls away. Low-lying furniture, such as futons and coffee tables, are also preferable to high-backed chairs and tables, since they will keep your visual horizon clear and help to maintain a spacious feeling.

Modular furniture multiplies your choices. Three small tables can act separately as a sideboard, work surface and bedside table, or they can be joined together to make a large dining table. Fold up a table so that it lies flat against a wall or stack chairs and hang them from a hook on the wall. Roll away a futon at the beginning of the day to convert a sleeping space into a work room. Use open, movable shelving that reaches from floor to ceiling to maximize the space you need for books and mementos.

Finally, if all else fails, use mirrors to artificially expand your space. But take note of some old words of wisdom: moderation is far better than excess.

< one-room living

High ceilings that allow for "stacking" or platform space are the key to having all your living areas in just one large room. Try to keep your home as clutter free as possible because this will help to prevent you from feeling crowded by your possessions.

Basement living

Often poorly decorated and underperforming, basements suffer from a lack of light, a propensity to leak water and are often cold year-round. Even so, with a little imagination and careful improvement you can convert them into comfortable and low-energy additional living spaces.

WARM AND LIGHT

The first step to successful basement living is to fix damp and cold spots with appropriate water-proofing and insulation. Strip out old carpets, since these might be concealing damp and holding in dust and mold. Repair damp patches and insulate old windows with weather stripping and thick curtains. The next step is to select a color scheme that is both warming and light. Warmer wall finishes are suitable, particularly in living spaces where a plain white finish might not attract enough natural daylight to feel really welcoming.

Basement spaces usually have concrete floors, which make them very cold in winter. To achieve a warmer effect, both visually and physically, use a softer floor covering, such as linoleum. Alternatively you can seal the concrete with a rubber finish (adding comfort and colour with rugs), or lay an inch of insulation on the floor and cover this with a light wood floor, which will retain the warmth from your heating system, preventing its loss to the ground underneath.

Finally, try to pay as much attention to the outside perimeter of your basement space as you do to the inside. Render courtyards with a light mineral plaster or decorate the area with bright ceramic tiles. Link these outside spaces with your interior space with the use of plants or common materials (use the same ceramic tiles inside and out, for example), which will give the illusion of expanding the edges of your home.

> ### making an entrance
This below-ground space benefits from light-colored walls, large windows and an arched roof with exposed beams, giving the illusion of greater height.

> ### dining downstairs
If the structure of your home allows, consider knocking out the walls in your basement to maximize the amount of light circulating. Open up the external walls as much as possible, too, to enhance your connection with the world just outside your windows.

Attics

In a crowded metropolis, one of the best places to live is on the top floor. Here you will receive more light, breathe cleaner air and have better, sometimes even panoramic, views.

Not all of us have the option to live in a high-rise building, however, let alone its top floor. But don't despair! You can still get the benefits of a warm, light-filled and resource-efficient space by carefully thinking through your options in order to convert your attic.

v peaceful productivity
A study in the loft has the unique benefits of being warm, private and peaceful. This space can get hot at midday, but blinds will help to reduce the temperature, as well as any glare.

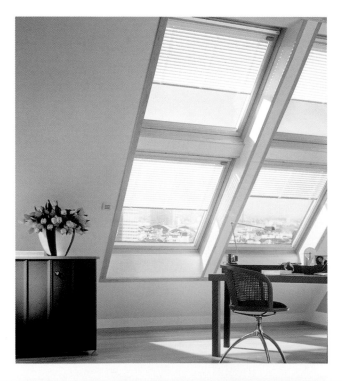

PLANNING
Loft living will work best if there is a south- or west-facing aspect to the space. If this isn't possible, then plan to convert the roof so that it has a sun-facing window with a low base that can be opened in summer. This way the whole of the attic room becomes an extension of the outdoors.

Use the gable ends or create flat-roofed loft extensions so that standard vertical windows can be installed. A number of smaller windows on two or three exterior walls will create views all around and enable you to receive even and varied natural light wherever you are in the space. Generally windows installed in the pitch of the roof are prone to leaks, may give poor views of the horizon and, if they face sunward, cause overheating in summer while letting in little solar warmth in winter. The example at the left uses blinds to control the temperature.

> the high life
If storage is a problem in your home, converting the attic will provide a good, practical solution. Shelving units will fit snugly under eaves and wall partitions can double as extra wardrobe space.

Conservatories

This room is the ideal place between indoors and outdoors, between nature and our modern world. In summer, its open doors and windows allow the garden to seep into the house, while in the winter the conservatory acts as an extra blanket against the winter cold.

The main benefit of conservatories is that they provide cheap additional living space in the warmer months of the year. In addition, they can act as draft lobbies and, surrounded by growing plants and simple natural materials, make the perfect spot to spend time relaxing first thing in the morning or last thing at night. A solar conservatory will also provide simple heat storage.

SUITABLE LOCATIONS

The best direction for a solar conservatory is facing south. However, an east- or west-facing room will also collect warmth and provide extra

> **additional rooms**
Building a conservatory onto your home will not only offer the benefit of letting in natural light, but it may also create much-needed space for a summer dining room.

insulation to your home. A west-facing room stays warm well into the evening, while an east-facing room provides warmth until mid-afternoon. Avoid a shady outlook that blocks the sun's heat, and make sure your conservatory is constructed with a solid insulated floor and an airtight wood and glass structure above.

In cold climates, the conservatory roof and walls should be double glazed to prevent frost. In warm climates, the entire structure can be single glazed, with a solid west wall and external roof shades to prevent the space from over-heating in summer.

Never heat a conservatory artificially and always separate it from your living room by double-glazed windows and doors. Otherwise it will only add to your home's energy costs. This may seem unreasonable, particularly on a winter's day when it will be too cold to spend time there comfortably, but this is the reality of living with the seasons. In any case, a true solar space should always have the smell of the outside air and the character of external materials.

cool space

Conservatories can get very hot in the summer months. One way to drop the temperature is to create shade, either by growing creeping vines (left) or by installing conservatory blinds (above).

AN INDOOR GARDEN

Suffused with light, conservatories are ideal spaces for growing plants. As well as stimulating your senses by providing color and perfume, plants can help to absorb certain pollutants in the home (see page 31), purify the air by replacing carbon dioxide with oxygen and also provide your home with salads, fruits and herbs.

People
and pets

While eco-ideas work across generations, we are all individuals with differing needs. We age, acquire new things, share, meet a partner, have a child perhaps, discover new abilities and new disabilities, grow older than our bones might wish, and move from the city to the country and then back again. Each change brings with it a new challenge, and the possibility of enriching our lives through careful choices. To make an eco-friendly home you therefore need to consider designs that work across generations, that can adapt to change without becoming obsolete or unwanted. Choose furniture and fixtures designed for all and remember that your home will need to house many eventualities, from home-working and child-care to helping the old or the sick.

Chapter Five

Babies

As every parent knows, babies are affected by the world around them long before they are born: the chemicals in the air and in our food all affect the nurturing environment that is the womb.

To give your baby the best start in life, avoid smoky environments and remove heavily processed food from your diet. Take advantage of the nesting instinct by researching local sources of secondhand baby furniture and clothes and preparing an eco-friendly nursery.

WHICH ROOM IS BEST?

Careful consideration is required when you are choosing a room in your home for your baby's nursery. It should be warm and cozy with enough space for a crib, clothing and diaper changing. Ideally, the room should be big enough so that the crib can be replaced by a bed for a young child. Choose neutral colors that won't overwhelm your baby and concentrate color and sound in simple playthings that are safe to leave in the crib or suspend overhead.

Newborns cannot regulate their body temperature, so it is very important to make sure that the nursery has a good supply of heat (room temperature should be a uniform 67 to 69°F), with draft-free windows and heavy curtains or blinds that also serve to block

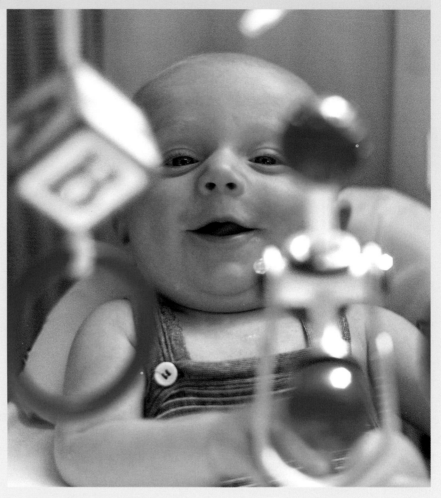

∧ **simple delights**

Babies are very easily amused, so entertain them with whatever it is you have on hand. Mobiles are an old favorite; you can even make your own with bright-colored objects that vary in shape and form.

out light. Since babies are highly sensitive to changes in light, a dimmer switch is ideal for the nursery. Alternatively, use lampshades to create soft, unobtrusive lighting. All electrical and gas fittings should be well maintained, so make sure that any old fixtures, plugs and appliances are checked by a qualified electrician or plumber.

If you are intending to redecorate the nursery, consider choosing a chemically inert paint (see pages 66–68), and remove carpets to reduce the amount of trapped dust and dust mites.

EQUIPPING THE NURSERY

Newborns grow very quickly so a lot of baby furniture is used only for a limited period of time. This is one very good reason to use secondhand furniture made from eco-friendly timber.

If you do buy new furniture, make sure you choose objects that are made from natural materials. Also, look for furniture that grows with your baby rather than sits unwanted in the attic after only a few months of use.

Another option is to adapt existing furniture to suit the nursery, rather than buying items specially designed for your baby. A chest of drawers with a mat and side rails on top, for example, can easily double as a changing table. A comfortable low chair can be moved from the living room into the nursery for breast-feeding. Simple wool rugs with nonslip backing strips can be placed on the floor to let your baby toddle around in comfort.

Similarly, be creative with other baby paraphernalia. Rather than buying a special sterilizing appliance, just sterilize bottles in a saucepan with a lid.

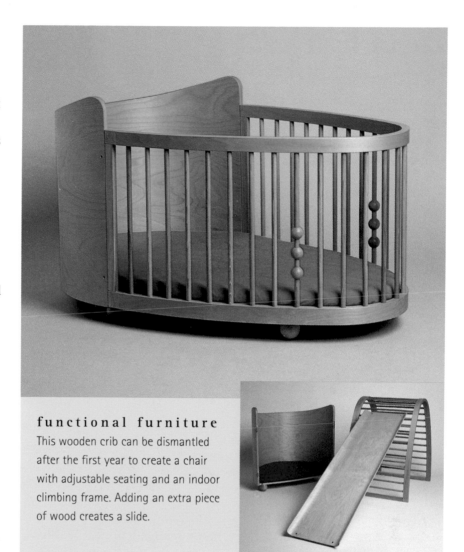

functional furniture
This wooden crib can be dismantled after the first year to create a chair with adjustable seating and an indoor climbing frame. Adding an extra piece of wood creates a slide.

BABY TOYS

There are two approaches to buying baby toys. The first is to buy them as an instantaneous amusement fix, and the second is to buy them with a view to their becoming treasured objects that last a lifetime and beyond. Unaffected by the powers of marketing and advertising, most babies are at their happiest playing with simple household objects that create sound, such as jangling a set of keys, banging pots and pans with wooden spoons or crumpling up soft tissue paper or newspaper. The store-bought, brightly colored, noisy battery-run plastic contraptions will also keep your

< fun with food
Babies love playing with food, and will find great delight in helping you to prepare meals. Introduce your children early to the pleasures of fresh, organic produce and you will help them to establish a healthy attitude to food.

Eternally yours: the toy box

If this is your first baby, consider buying a large, solid wooden box to store all your children's toys. Not only will this serve its purpose during baby- and toddlerhood but it will also be a useful piece of furniture for years to come. Use it to store linen, old files and anything else that you want to keep but don't need to be readily accessible. You can even make one yourself.

BABY CLOTHES

Because babies grow very quickly, newborn clothes are only worn for a very short time. Friends and family members who have already had babies are a good source of relatively new hand-me-down sweaters, jumpers, socks, mittens, baby bonnets and bibs, so make sure to ask them for any cast-offs before you buy a brand-new baby wardrobe. Alternatively, keep your baby's clothes for your next baby, or offer them to friends who are about to start a family.

If you do buy secondhand clothes for your baby, choose ones that are made from natural materials, such as cotton, and make sure that they are free of chemicals. This will help to protect your baby's skin from allergic reactions until she or he has built up a natural resistance to the world and its surroundings.

baby entertained but will, most likely, eventually end up unwanted in a pile somewhere, either broken or out-of-date. If you do decide to buy manufactured toys for your baby, look for well-made, solid, durable and imaginative items made from natural materials that can be dismantled easily. These can then become a set of building blocks as your baby's dexterity gradually develops.

v eco-toys
Always try to choose toys made from sustainable materials, such as wood, and make sure the paints used to decorate them are nontoxic. Soft toys should always have hypoallergenic fillings.

DIAPERS

One of the biggest questions having to do with babies is whether you should buy disposables or join the cotton club. While the original cotton diaper was rough, bulky, leaky and hard to change, the modern equivalents (when used with diaper covers) are sleek, soft, watertight and use NASA-approved Velcro for quick release. Some even have micro-fiber covers that allow your baby's skin to breathe.

Over the first two years of your baby's life, you will use at least two thousand disposable diapers, all of which are manufactured from highly treated cotton and plastic. They are bleached and, more recently, filled with ecologically dubious liquid-absorbing gels, and they are also difficult to dispose of safely. Reusable diapers, on the other hand, can last for a decade and, if washed in bulk and dried on the line, use less energy than the mass-marketed alternative. Better

still, hire a local diaper service that will collect your used diapers, wash them in bulk and return them clean weekly.

Midway between the two ends of the diaper war are the flushable (or compostable) liners, cotton diapers and waterproof pants. These are ideal for when you and your baby are traveling away from home.

MADE IN NORWAY

Adaptable chairs

Manufactured in Norway, these solid wooden chairs are made from cultivated beech. The height and depth of the seat and footrest can be adjusted, so they are ideal items of furniture for a growing child. The seat can elevate to the height of the table, ensuring that your children are sitting at the right height for the table with their feet supported at the same time. With extra cushioning and a safety harness, they make appropriate high chairs for babies aged between six and twelve months who can support their heads. The enduring quality of the wood means that teenagers and adults will also be able to sit comfortably on them.

Children

Once weaned, out of diapers and in their own room, kids are a bundle of laughs, frights, cares and despairs in equal measure. Between the ages of three and thirteen your children learn more about the world around them than they will learn in the rest of their lives. Many of these adventures and learning experiences will happen in the privacy of their own bedroom, away from the organizing rigor and limiting imagination of parents. The key requirement for a child's bedroom is that it should be a haven for imagination and growth. However, you should also cover the practical matters of comfort and safety.

ALLOCATING ROOMS
Children will play, sleep, dress and do homework in their bedroom, so don't try to to squeeze them into the smallest room in your home. Where possible, choose a room that is large enough for all these needs

> totally engrossed
One of the joys of childhood is being able to live in a world of make-believe. For a parent, the benefit of this is that you don't have to buy the latest toys. With a little imagination (both yours and your child's!) simple, well-made toys provide just as much fun.

or, if you have two or more children, consider giving them smaller sleeping rooms with a separate room to house all their toys and in which to play with their friends.

For everyone's sake, a child's bedroom should be separate from the parents'. If you want to keep an ear on your kids when they are small, install a wire-free baby monitor in their room. Make sure you take it out before they realize that you're eavesdropping, by which time they'll be old enough to take care of themselves.

Safety first
For safety, you may want to choose a bedroom on the ground floor to reduce the danger of the child falling downstairs but, alternatively, a child's bedroom upstairs means you don't have to tiptoe around the house after early-evening bedtimes. If you do opt for upstairs, make sure that you have a well-secured handrail and that the surface you choose to cover the stairs isn't too slippery.

FURNITURE
When possible, always choose oversized furniture: big beds and

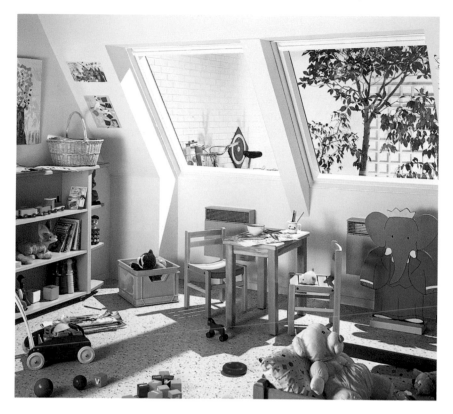

< neutral colors
Ideally, the color scheme for a kid's bedroom should be pale or neutral because this will allow for more flexibility as your child's tastes develop and change.

can cope with the increased demand. If space is a problem, bunk beds are one good solution, but make sure the child in the bottom bunk can sit up comfortably without hitting his head on the top bunk. Another separate but compact alternative is to screen off the area around the bed for some privacy, but maintain a common dressing and play area. This arrangement should work well until the teen years arrive.

DECORATIONS

A simple combination of colors and materials will provide a good backdrop for your kids' own imagination and endure the fads that came and go throughout the years.

When the time comes your children won't hesitate to plaster their bedroom walls with images

chairs are great fun for kids because they provide far more opportunity for play than tiny stools and beds. They'll also last longer and form part of your child's personal possessions as they grow. Wood makes warm and robust furniture, while steel tubular furniture with fabric covers is colder to the touch but lighter and therefore easier to move around.

Obviously, the cabinets, desks and dressers you choose should be designed so they can actually be used by children, but consider building shelves, first at a low level, then adding upward to match both your child's height and increasing number of toys, clothes and books.

Colorful plastic storage boxes are light, cheap and sturdy, so they are

perfect for holding toys at the end of the day.

For wardrobes, buy ones that close securely, to protect clothes from dust and moths. They will also give your kids' rooms a semblance of tidiness.

At an early age, kids love to share their rooms with their brothers and sisters because it provides them with security and playmates. But beyond the ages of eight or nine, they may start to want their own space and you will have to see whether your home

> soft edges
The corners of tables and other sharp edges often fall at children's head height, so they may pose a danger. To avoid this, attach plastic corner bumpers.

of their favorite pop and TV stars, but this is far better than your imposing a color scheme or heavily patterned design to the room that will age even more quickly in a rapidly growing child's eyes.

Keep a cork bulletin board on the wall to stick up favorite pictures or schoolwork, and maybe keep another wall free for your children to paint however they feel suits them best each year. Blackboard paint on part of a wall is another good option.

Floors in a child's bedroom are best being soft and easy to clean. Linoleum is preferable to installed carpets, and any rugs should have nonslip backing in order to

∧ **riding the wave of technology**
As your children grow older, they'll definitely want to be part of the digital age. In addition to being fun and educational, small portable computers also consume very little energy and space.

prevent accidental slipping. For safety's sake, keep furniture away from window sills and install a window stop so that they can't open more than a hand's width. Fabric roller shades make good window screens; they hold less dust and are less likely to be broken than wooden blinds.

ECOLOGICAL TOYS

Any plaything that is adaptable, multifunctional, nontoxic, made from tough renewable materials and long lasting can be considered an eco-toy. Unfortunately, many modern toys are designed either to be instant fixes or part of a collectible series that's fashionable one year but disappears the next. These encourage closets full of junk that nobody wants and a kid screaming out for more—not a pretty sight! The following are just some of the many eco-options, so

set some basic parameters and see if your kids can lead the way!

Froebel toys
The German educationalist Friedrich Froebel created a series of eight gifts that formed a basic part of his "earth-centered" educational ideas. The gifts start as simple playthings that help kids to see and understand basic shapes and textures like soft spheres and hard cubes, then they grow into building blocks and frameworks, eventually providing the basis for hobbies such as embroidery, modeling and mat-weaving.

Cut and paste
Kids love cutting out pictures from last week's magazine and pasting them into scrapbooks, so keep a good supply of nontoxic glue, paints, pencils and scissors. Every time the old scrapbook runs out of

room, buy a new one, and encourage your child to make collages of color and do some play-writing in it every once in a while. In years to come, these will serve as a diary of sorts that you and your kids can treasure. Similarly, set aside a box in which to keep old wrapping paper, egg cartons and toilet-paper rolls and encourage them to make their own playthings.

Outdoor sports

Whether the preference is football, tennis, hockey or rugby, ball games keep your children fit. Encourage your children to invite friends over to play, which will help them to get out of the house and away from the TV. Sports have turned into big business, but all in all they are far better than war!

A bike is also a great idea and probably the first bit of freedom that a child can receive. If you are worried about the local streets

> solar powered
Buying radios and other electrical equipment that are powered by the sun will curb the need for disposable and nonrecyclable batteries.

being dangerous and polluted, then start complaining to your city council now, and get your kids involved it in too!

Electronic games

There are plenty of cautions that apply to this medium, but, overall, it is possible to see the ecological benefits through the haze of mass-produced electronics. If you choose wisely, items such as an Internet-connected portable computer or solar-powered radio can provide hours of fun and learning without consuming vast amounts of energy or materials. In eco-design this is called dematerialization—matter disappearing and being replaced by "pure" communication.

Old favorites

Chess, Scrabble, playing cards and dominoes are among the few games that last forever, and they are guaranteed to entertain and educate your children well into their teenage years and adulthood. If you can afford it, choose the well-made versions, which may even outlast your kids, who can give them to their own children.

< lifelong pursuits
Give your children a means to focus their natural inquisitiveness by encouraging them to take up a hobby, such as learning a musical instrument.

Teenagers

By this time, your children will be independent, aware and often cranky. Everyone needs their own space and teenagers are no different. They also have their own ideas of how space should be decorated and maintained. Some teenagers are clumsy, messy and liable to break anything within their reach. Others are tidy to the point of neurosis. Most, however, fall somewhere in between and could do with some help in deciding how to furnish their rooms.

NECESSITIES

As well as reflecting his or her general taste, a teenager's bedroom should have adequate space for studying. This means a desk (preferably with drawers), a comfortable chair and lots of shelving for storing books.

Teenagers will want to use their rooms to entertain friends, so make sure there is enough space for this. A low bed is good for lounging on, but consider also large floor cushions or beanbags.

Choose well-made, tough furniture that is also mobile. This allows them to move things around as their needs and tastes change. You may be able to buy well-made desks at knock-down prices from schools or offices that are refurbishing. Also, consider that your teenage children may take their bedroom furniture with them when they leave home. To make sure they will be happy doing this, discuss your furniture choices together and involve them in the purchasing process.

Listening to loud music is an inevitable part of teenage life, so for everyone's sake make sure your teenager's room is well insulated. If there is space, build cabinets on either side of the door. Filled with books and other belongings, this will act as an acoustic barrier between the teenager's room and the rest of the house.

If the room has enough height, you can build a high-level platform for a futon or mattress and the space underneath can act as a work or music den. Alternatively, you can use this space for extra storage.

< peace and privacy
Teenagers will invariably spend hours chatting on the telephone, so make sure they have the comfort, privacy and means to do this in their own bedrooms.

Young adults

During our twenties, most of us are determined to work hard and play hard, which leaves little time to think about the damage we wreak on the environment. Food is fast, convenient and throwaway; fashion is up-to-date and disposable; and furniture is cheap, cheerful and short-lived. Living in tune with the planet doesn't mean dropping out of this modern lifestyle, however. All we need to do is look before we leap.

FURNITURE

Most of our furniture requirements are just as appropriate when we are young as when we are old. But we do need to pay extra attention to certain matters at this stage in our lives. Because we are often on the move, the best way of making things last is to purchase small, portable and tough furniture that we can lug from place to place with relative ease. This doesn't have to mean uncomfortable or plain: a multicolored wool rug can be rolled up and lain out anywhere; futons and wood bases can be rearranged a dozen times to function as bedding, coffee tables or a couch. Equally, don't be caught up in convention: stack a pile of totally unrelated secondhand shelves on top of each other and fill them with your favorite things. As well as being a cool composition of your own, this will be just as cheap as

∧ flat sharing
Getting a job and moving out of the parental home combine to make the early twenties an incredibly exciting time. Make a habit of shopping and cooking together with your roommates because it's cheaper and more fun and it will save energy too.

poorly made furniture but last far longer.

ECOLOGICAL AWARENESS

If you are renting, it is unlikely that you'll be able to afford, let alone feel responsible for, improving the energy efficiency of your home over the long term. Despite this, you can undertake very simple measures to do your part for your home and the planet. Adding weather stripping, installing temporary plastic-wrap double glazing and buying low-energy bulbs that you can take with you are all cheap and easy solutions that will decrease your utility bills. Instead of turning up the thermostat on cold winter days, get in touch with the seasons and wear socks and an extra sweater instead. Whenever you leave a room, remember to turn off the lights, and whenever you go away for the weekend, turn off the heating.

Older adults

It is only when we reach our later years that we discover the worth of our possessions. As we look back on our lives, we find that the things we treasure most are simple and long lasting—friends, a perfect view, memories of life events, a favorite record or a tree planted forty years ago that is now grown and gnarled.

Reflection also involves looking around you at the big house you have occupied over the past years, the rooms where children have played and screamed, the double garage, and the neat suburban neighborhood that many of us find ourselves in. Looking toward the future includes planning for retirement, welcoming grandchildren and, let's be honest, facing the onset of frailty and our eventual demise.

DOWNSIZING

When the children have flown the nest, it is time to reconsider your household needs and desires and repackage yourself so that you can really do more with less.

For some, downsizing involves selling the big family home, with the big energy and maintenance bills, and finding a smaller

dwelling. Perhaps a small, easily maintained pad in the city where you can entertain will suit your new needs. If the city smog is getting you down and green fields beckon, find a cottage in your favorite small village, where the post office and the pub are still the places where people gather.

When your home no longer supports a growing family, this is the time to replace large-scale, energy-consuming appliances, such as a four- or six-burner stove, with those that are designed for just one or two. In essence, aim to reconfigure your life so that it flows with the world around you.

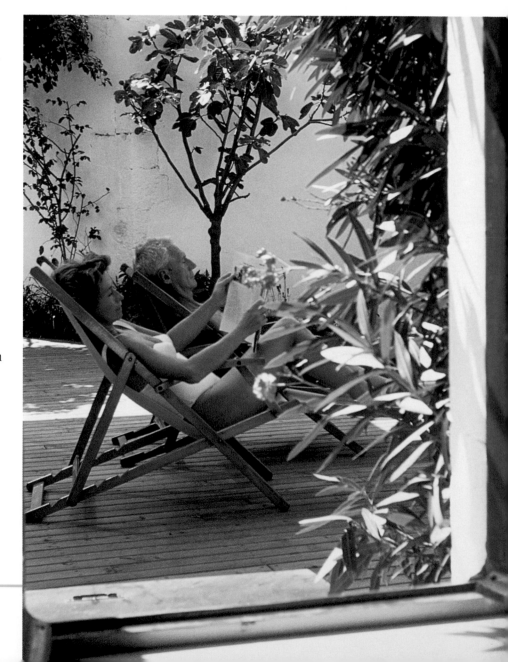

> **low maintenance**
Once children leave home, a large lawn may not be as important, so consider a courtyard with wood decking instead.

> special needs

This kitchen is specially designed for those with reduced mobility. It features taps that are easy to turn on and off, low-level sinks with wheelchair access and mobile storage units that also double as work spaces.

For others, downsizing may simply involve a careful review of daily habits. Good insulation and thick curtains will keep your heating bills low, as will turning down thermostats and closing heater vents in unused rooms. Likewise, turning the lights off when they are not needed and using electrical appliances wisely will cut down on your electricity bills. Taking in lodgers is another way of ensuring that your home and its resources aren't wasted.

If you have the time, consider taking up a practical hobby, such as sewing or woodworking. This way you'll be able to mend or repair a worn or broken item instead of just replacing it.

DESIGNING FOR DISABILITY

Even if we are in good health, we should always consider the needs of others and make our homes more user-friendly for those who are less physically able. Many countries now have legislation for new housing to meet minimum standards of accessibility.

Basic requirements
One of the basic needs of disabled people is to have enough space to move around key parts of the home in a wheelchair. For this reason, make sure doorways have flat or only slightly graded access. They should also be at least 3 feet wide with a clear opening.

Any stairs in your home should have comfortable handrails beside them. A contrasting floor covering on each step will also make stairs easily visible to those with poor eyesight.

Easy access to bathrooms is critical, since it can take more time to reach these rooms if you are

less steady on your feet. If possible, have a toilet on each floor of your home, particularly the ground floor.

Facilities in the bathroom should include a wide shower space with a fold-up seat, an adjustable shower head and vertical and horizontal handrails for support.

As we grow older, our joints may become stiffer and our muscles weaker. To accommodate this, replace soft, low-slung easy chairs with firm chairs that have straight backs. Taps with lever arms will also be easier to use than those with more traditional screw fittings.

< less is more

Later life is the time to downsize, so if you are still driving a spacious, gas-guzzling car, consider alternatives, such as the high-efficiency "smart" car.

Pets

Not only are pets good companions, but they also keep us in touch with nature in the simple act and pleasure of caring for another creature. Despite this, they are not a simple addition to an eco-friendly home, and the larger they are, the more space, care and attention they need.

SPACE CONSIDERATIONS

Only choose a large pet, such as a dog, if you have plenty of space in your home and, ideally, a large backyard. You will also need to have time available to give your dog free access to the outside world because, just like humans, dogs get tired of their own four fences. In comparison, cats make better pets in an urban environment because they are more able to care for themselves and less likely to be upset when left to their own devices.

Smaller pets, such as hamsters and rabbits, are normally kept in cages to prevent them from getting lost or fouling the home and, as a result, they live a dull and mundane existence in a trapped environment. You and your children may think they are cute and entertaining, but they really would prefer to be out there in the big, wide world, and for this reason they are not recommended.

A more ecologically minded approach to pets is to keep them for their usefulness. Chickens, for example, will happily eat most kitchen scraps as well as produce

∨ **clean and happy**
Teach your children to wash their hands and faces after handling pets and opt for wood flooring rather than carpets because these are easier to clean.

< faithful companions
If you live on your own, caring for a pet can give you a sense of purpose and belonging. Cats make good pets in cities because they are independent and don't need much space.

application of over-the-counter medication, you may want to ask your vet about further treatment with prescription medicine.

PET FOOD

The majority of pet food comes from industrialized slaughterhouses, and it seems quite irrational of animal lovers to feed their pets the output of these slaughterhouses. There are plenty of alternative cereal and nutrient-based pet foods, which are not only much better for your pets' digestion but also better for the environment in general. If you want to take pet food a step further, make your own from dining table leftovers.

eggs and manure. A tethered sheep will keep your lawn trimmed beautifully and provide an annual fleece of wool, while a pond filled with carp will stimulate a complex water eco-system and encourage a balanced mix of pond life. Check with local authorities to see if the animal you are considering may legally be kept within your city.

HYGIENE CONSIDERATIONS

Most pets are relatively clean by their own nature. However, they aren't as careful or as discriminating as we might hope and a home that includes a pet will undoubtedly require more cleaning than a home without. To make the task a little easier, choose wall and floor coverings that are easy to clean (see pages 56–64).

Homes with pets will also have a greater risk of infestation from pests, such as fleas, mites and ticks. To avoid pet-derived illness, train your children to wash their hands and faces after playing with their pets, and regularly check both your children and your pets for signs of fleas and other undesirables. If your pet's infestation doesn't clear up with

> lifestyle compatible
If there is little space in your home or you don't have a lot of time, you should choose a low-maintenance pet, such as a goldfish.

Allergies

At some point in his or her life, one in ten people will experience an allergy. This is when the body's defense mechanism becomes hypersensitive and forms antibodies against a substance that is innocuous to most people.

DIFFERENT ALLERGIES

There are three different types of allergies: airborne, contact and food allergies. Airborne allergies are caused when we breathe in air that contains small dust or pollen particles or chemicals released by natural and synthetic materials. Contact allergies are skin reactions to materials as diverse as the copper and nickel found in coins and jewelry, and synthetic chemicals such as formaldehyde, epoxy resin or thiuram found in cosmetics, rubber and reconstituted wood.

Scientists believe that most people will eventually react adversely to the chemically complex soup that makes up the modern living and working environment. By removing problem materials from the home and workplace, we can minimize the risk. Yet, concern for an allergy-free environment should not become an unhealthy obsession. Instead, aim to create a balance between accepting the world around you and realistically combating polluting sources.

PREVENTING ALLERGIES

To reduce the risk of developing or suffering from an allergy, aim to create a dry, dust-free and well-ventilated home. Remove carpets and opt for hard flooring instead. To prevent dirt and dust from accumulating in the home, wipe floors down regularly with a slightly damp cloth, close windows facing onto polluted streets and take off your shoes at the front door. Since damp air and surfaces are a haven for microbes, make

ECO-TIP

A night in the cooler
Some experts believe that the common house mite is the cause of over half of all asthma cases. As tiny as grains of sand, dust mites thrive in bedding and carpets by feeding on sloughed-off human skin cells that accumulate there. The Scandinavians get rid of these bugs by washing and drying bedding, then hanging it out to air during the winter night. The freezing temperatures kill the mites. In warmer climates the same results can be achieved by putting your pillow and duvet covers in the freezer overnight.

sure you address any moisture problems in your home (see pages 31–32). In wet and humid climates you may have to buy a dehumidifier to deal with excessively damp air. You can also install a whole-house heat recovery ventilation system to filter home air and reduce dust and chemical buildup (see page 40).

Choosing solid wood furnishings instead of heavily upholstered ones will also help, as will regularly washing fabrics and throws. Avoid having flowers, trees and plants that are pollinated by the wind, such as daisies, marigolds, willows and birch, near your home; select instead plants pollinated by insects and birds, such as fruit trees, sweet-smelling flowers and herbs.

Since homes are becoming increasingly airtight, it is also very important to select general household materials and cleaning products that are beneficial or not harmful to your health. For more information on ecological cleaning products see page 165.

∧ **simple measures**
One way to avoid allergies is to keep plants in and around your home that are pollinated by birds and insects, such as herbs and fruit trees, rather than those that are pollinated by the wind.

< **clean and hypoallergenic**
Dust and house mites thrive in bedding, so change your sheets regularly. Using fabrics that are hypoallergenic will also help to prevent allergies.

Upkeep

Literally and figuratively, the home is a protective and nurturing shell, and how we care for it has a direct bearing on how we care for ourselves and our planet. Each layer of the home—from its structure, insulation and utilities to the personal possessions inside—can and should be maintained in an ecologically minded way that improves the health, quality and feel of our space and therefore our own general well-being. Consider the three r's (reduce, reuse, recycle) and learn to spot potential problems before they envelop you.

Chapter Six

Maintenance and repair

The usual response to maintenance is a groan at the time, effort and expense involved, but each time you discover a problem try instead to see it as an opportunity to improve your home. Don't just make do and mend; think the problem through and devise a better, longer-lasting solution. A window is old and leaky, but it has a great view into your garden. Maximize this by replacing it with a modern double-glazed, wood-framed French window that opens onto the garden. You will not only be replacing the window but also creating an alternative route outside and increasing the amount of light in your home. By improving as you maintain, you'll find the whole home-maintenance experience much more rewarding.

OUTSIDE THE HOME

The ground outside your home can pretty much look after itself provided that it is well drained and stable. Keep outside drains clear to prevent flooding and get a plumber to inspect manholes every few years to check that the brick-work down there is still sound. Similarly, if you plan on doing a lot of digging in your garden, take care because underground cables and pipes are often poorly marked and if you accidentally damage them, there may be disruptive and dangerous consequences.

Drainage

If the area around your home becomes waterlogged after heavy rains, this means your drainage is either blocked or inadequate. To improve drainage, either increase the size and number of drains around your home or create drainage channels at ground level that will draw rainwater away from the foundation walls. On larger properties you can even build a pond or water meadow to collect excess water. At the same time you will be creating an ecologically valuable and beautiful habitat. A landscape architect or engineer will be able to run through all the options with you.

If you live in a particularly wet climate, place a border of hard, well-draining bricks along the side of your home. This will be a practical and attractive solution

∧ **planning prevention pays**
Like people, buildings can either grow old gracefully or fall apart at the seams rather disgracefully. Whatever you do, don't postpone maintenance because it doesn't get any easier and the longer you leave it, the worse it gets.

and will work much better than poorly draining flower beds would.

Tree maintenance

Above the ground, prune tall trees to prevent them from becoming too top-heavy and toppling over in high winds. Trees that are not on your property but whose branches hang over your side of the fence should also be tackled. In general, tall trees close to your home are best avoided because their roots burrow deep in search of water and can eventually cause damage to the foundations.

If your home is built on clay soils (ones that absorb water and expand or contract when dry) then trees growing close to your home will be even more of a problem. Broad-leaved trees or trees that grow quickly require a lot of water and consequently grow large root systems that spread outward in search of water. You can't necessarily tell which trees will cause a problem so monitor the garden and walls for signs of movement and call in a building contractor if you are concerned. Large or older trees are sometimes protected by preservation laws so you may have to ask your city council for permission to remove dangerous trees or pollard them (see eco-tip box, right).

Subsidence

If you notice cracks in the external walls of your home, this may be a sign of subsidence caused by shrinking soil or weak foundations. Underpinning, which comprises digging down to the base of the foundations and providing additional support, is an expensive but necessary measure if soil movement around your home is substantial.

PROTECTING YOUR FRAMEWORK

Rain, wind and sun are all pernicious forces that, unmanaged, can do great damage to your home. Rainwater can seep in unnoticed, rotting wood or rusting steel. High winds can destroy a poorly constructed home, tearing away siding and ripping up poorly fixed tiles. The sun heats up surfaces, making them expand and contract every day and night,

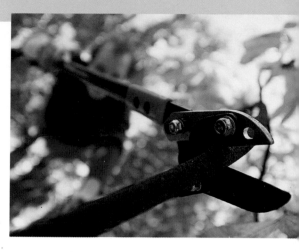

∧ **pruning**
Regularly lop off the branches of tall trees so that leaves and twigs don't find their way into gutters and drainpipes.

which can eventually weaken and damage the underlying structure, allowing water and air to leak inside.

Gutters and downpipes

To protect your home against water damage, check and clear rooftop gutters and downspouts twice a year. Even if there are no tall trees near your house, birds may decide to make a sheltered gutter into a nest and cause blockage. See that gutters are still firmly secured to roofs and that pipes are securely bolted to the wall of your home. Roof tiles and flashing should also be checked at least once a year to see if there are any cracks or drips. At the first sign of damage, fix the problem. Otherwise it will grow exponentially until you have no choice but to repair it and by that

> ### ECO-TIP
>
> **Stemming tree roots**
> One way to prevent trees from damaging your house is to pollard them. This common procedure stops the roots of trees from growing by cutting its branches back to the trunk. A pollarded tree grows straight, thin branches that can be used to make fences or provide renewable heating in the countryside.

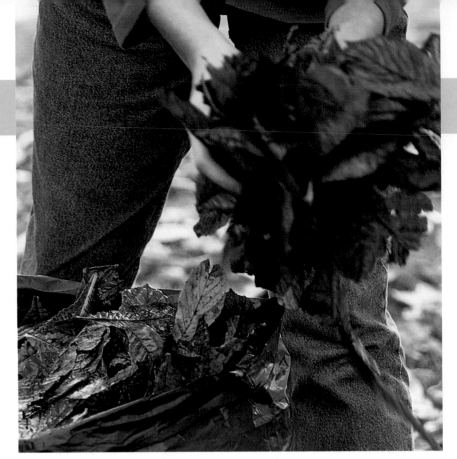

> **weekend chores**
Leaves and other garden mulch will trap water and create damp, so regularly sweep or rake up around the outside walls of your home to keep them clear.

stage it will usually be at a high cost. If your gutters do need replacing, choose polypropylene piping since this is cheaper and longer lasting than metal or wood alternatives. You can also cover gutters with wire mesh to prevent leaves from falling in. While you're at it, connect the downspouts to a tank and reuse this water in and around your home.

Paintwork

Most external wood and metal work needs repainting every five to ten years to protect it from the elements. Wooden window and door frames, external siding and fascia panels are all vulnerable to the elements and should be checked yearly for signs of peeling paint, warping or rot. When it is time to repaint, consider whether a color change might improve the feel of your home and neighborhood (see page 66).

External walls

Solid brick walls will also suffer from driving rain and cold temperatures, so examine these to make sure that the mortar is still filling the brick joints cleanly. If mortar is crumbling away, you will need to repoint the brickwork.

To prevent small repair jobs from turning into major undertakings, always keep an eye out for any signs of damage. In particular, check that walls are straight, that there are no cracks in the plaster and that roof lines are not sagging. If you have spotted signs of wear and tear, ask a contractor or engineer to examine them further because they may be signs of more serious, underlying problems, such as structural damage.

Problems can also arise if you take down walls or use furniture or floor coverings that are heavier than originally intended. Never make holes in external walls without seeking the advice of a professional and only remove internal walls if investigation shows that it is neither supporting weight from above nor stabilizing the building. Make sure that joists and walls can support the extra load from heavy furniture such as pianos or chunky flooring like terrazzo. If you find you do need to reinforce floors or walls, use secondary wood joists in preference to steel beams.

UTILITIES

Electricity, plumbing and gas are the hidden essentials of your home. When they fail you can end up with bills that far exceed the cost of maintaining them, so consider these invisibles in your home maintenance program.

Electricity

It's hard to be prescriptive about electrical systems, since standards and regulations vary from country to country. However, aim to minimize your demand by choosing low-energy appliances. This will also take some of the strain off cabling, fuses and power companies.

In older homes, cabling may be single-core with a rubberized fabric sheath, while appliance cords may be twin-core twisted cables with no earth protection. All these wires need replacing professionally because they are dangerous and could lead to fire or electric shock. If fuses or circuit breakers continuously blow for no apparent reason, you are either overloading the circuit or the cabling is damaged. Tell-tale signs include warm cabling or a distinct fishy smell; you should call in a qualified electrician to replace cabling.

When you move into a new property, you should always arrange to have electrical installations inspected to check and replace defective cables. A qualified electrician will also be able to check for damage caused by pests (who often chew through cables), broken or burnt-out sockets, unsheathed cables and overloaded circuits.

Annual maintenance measures you can do yourself include checking fuses or circuit breakers in your fuse box to make sure they are clean and operate properly, ensuring that outlets, appliance and lighting cables don't appear damaged, and testing and recharging batteries in smoke and carbon monoxide detectors.

Plumbing

Home plumbing is a major source of intermittent expense usually caused by accidental damage or ignoring obvious problems such as freezing pipes or dripping taps. If you do notice signs of leaking, always call the plumber right away rather than hoping the problem will suddenly disappear, because it won't! In any case, it's a good idea to call a plumber to your home every five years or so so that he or she can pressure test the heating and water systems and identify any leaks or weak fittings.

More regular checks that you can carry out yourself include making sure that the insulation on water pipes is a minimum of 1 inch, particularly in cold attics and basements. If you need to apply or replace the insulation, choose the eco-friendly alternatives of cork or cellulose insulation instead of foamed plastics. If you live in an older home, call your local water authority and ask them to conduct a water-quality test to make sure there is no trace of lead in your water supply.

If pipework needs changing, check with an experienced plumber to find out if your local plumbing code permits the use of plastic pipes (polypropylene can be used for both hot and cold systems), which are cheaper, longer lasting and less toxic than metal alternatives. If you fit plastic pipes between metal fittings, you must also install an earth bonding cable to conduct electrical charges to earth. To save energy, add thermostats and timer controls to heating systems while they undergo maintenance work.

In hard-water areas, limescale can build up inside water pipes, causing eventual blockage. To prevent or remove limescale in your plumbing system, you will need to use a hard-water filter, which you can buy in your local hardware store. Use lemon juice to remove limescale from shower heads by pouring the juice into a plastic bag and tying this around

∧ **clean and efficient**
To remove limescale, dismantle and leave all tap parts in a bowl of vinegar or lemon juice overnight. Rinse and refit the following day.

the shower head and leaving overnight. Citric acid crystals, which are available from chemical suppliers, are another option. A final eco-friendly option is to place magnets on either side of a hot water pipe. This will deactivate the limescale particles and prevent future buildup.

Prevent blockages by putting a garbage can next to the toilet for sanitary napkins, diapers and other toiletries and by using traps in showers, bathtubs and sinks. Never pour paints or fats into the drains. Instead, pour them into a jar and reuse them. Alternatively you can pour them onto some old newspapers and throw the soaked newspapers in the waste bin. Dispose of toxic paints according to requirements for hazardous waste disposal.

To unblock toilets, fill a bucket of water and stand on a seat so that you can pour it from a high level into the bowl. The force and quantity of the water should be enough to dislodge the blockage. If this doesn't work, pour boiling water into the bowl to soften or dissolve the waste matter, then use a plunger to force it clear.

Every now and again, fill bucket after bucket with used bathwater and pour it down the toilet. Bleach can be used as a final resort but choose the safer bleaches such as hydrogen peroxide instead of normal household bleach, because its active ingredients disperse quickly in the environment. Never mix household chemicals in an attempt to double the strength because they may react together to create toxic fumes.

Gas

All gas-fueled heating and cooking equipment needs regular maintenance to ensure that it is both safe and running efficiently. Most utility companies provide maintenance services that include checking to make sure that your systems are working properly. Gas appliances need to burn correctly

∧ **gas safety**
Carbon monoxide detectors installed next to gas appliances warn you of inadequate ventilation or damage to the burner. They can be bought from hardware shops.

and require effective ventilation to ensure that carbon monoxide does not build up in your home.

Gas burners need to be cleaned regularly because deposits will build up slowly and reduce the efficiency of the burner, leading to wasted energy. Maintaining your heater will save as much energy as will weatherproofing doors and windows. Also keep plants away from the heating vents to prevent poor burning or a fire.

< **fixing blockages**
In place of expensive, strong chemicals that are dangerous as well as polluting, simply use a plunger or hot water to remove blockages in your sink or toilet.

Household cleaning

Cleaning shouldn't be an exercise in germ warfare and, contrary to popular belief, a spotlessly clean home has the potential to be just as bad for us in the long run as a home with a little dust and the usual signs of human life. It's common knowledge that kids fare better if they grow up surrounded by other children with a rich mix of germs and illnesses, since this helps them to develop strong immune systems, that will fight against future infections. Rather than trying for 100 percent sterility, create a naturally healthy environment in your home using simple, nontoxic products.

FLOORS AND COVERINGS

Obviously, the type of floor you are cleaning will dictate the type of method you need to adopt. But, ultimately, you should be aiming to avoid getting your floors dirty in the first place. You can do this by using a big coir mat at the entrance of your home, taking shoes off at the front door and keeping spaghetti bolognese away from the carpet.

Wooden floors

A soft broom will remove most dust on wooden floors and a damp cloth will take care of the rest. If you follow a no-shoes policy in your home, you can even give your guests thick socks to walk around in and they'll polish your floor for free!

If your floors are sealed with linseed or wood oil stains, you will need to treat them again when the oils wear through; if they are unsealed, polish them every year

CLOSE-UP: NATURAL WAXES

Waxes, oils and thinners are produced naturally by trees and bees (and even in our ears) or can be synthesized from petrochemicals. Beeswax, tung tree oil, linseed oil, gum tree turpentine and citrus peel oil are relatively safe, while oil-derived products like paraffin wax, xylene and toluene are produced in high-energy processes with complex waste products. Beeswax is a good all-around polish that is easy to apply when thinned with odorless mineral spirits (the least toxic thinner available). You can also turn it into an effective wooden furniture cleaner by mixing it with vinegar.

or so with a good beeswax polish. Avoid using scrubbing brushes on wood floors, since the scratches increase the amount of dirt that collects on the surface. You should also avoid polyurethane varnishes that contain polyisocyanates, because these can cause irritation or allergic reactions. Only polish or refinish when it is really needed.

Concrete floors

If it is to remain clean, bare concrete needs to be sealed, which can be achieved by polishing with

> smooth sailing

Hard flooring need only be swept and washed with warm soapy water to stay clean. Avoid strong cleaners or rough scrubbing brushes, since these can pit or scratch the surface.

wax or sealing it with a paint or resin finish. Even low-odor resins give off toxic gases, so apply them in summer when you can open doors and windows to evaporate the solvent. Several layers of wax are needed to take away the hardness of untreated concrete but eventually it will glow warmly as it reflects the light.

Brick floors

If your floor is made of brick, it's best to allow the bricks to age naturally rather than plasticizing them with uncharacteristic sealants. Glazed tiles, mosaics and terrazzo can be left unsealed or treated with resin sealants, while unglazed tiles and slates can be polished with linseed oil and beeswax. Use rugs on hard flooring to keep your feet warm, or provide slippers for houseguests.

Soft floors

Linoleum, cork and other soft resilient floors need a gentle sweep

∧ HEPA filters

High-efficiency particulate air filters remove up to 99.9 percent of particles greater than 0.3 microns in diameter (a human hair is 100 microns thick) and can help in the fight against allergies.

and a light soapy wash to keep them clean. You will find that linoleum lasts longer if it is polished occasionally.

Installed carpets

These are literally the bugaboo in a clean home because they trap and hide dirt deep between the fibers. If you do have wall-to-wall carpets the best way to keep them dust free is to clean them once a week with a high-efficiency vacuum cleaner that has a ULPA or HEPA filter (see above).

For general carpet cleaning, dilute dishwashing liquid with

warm water and whip the mixture up into a light foam with a whisk. Sponge the foam into the carpet and wipe with a damp cloth. Odors can be reduced in carpets by airing regularly and sprinkling with bicarbonate of soda, followed, after a while, with a good vacuum. All carpets stain eventually, even those treated with proprietary stain guards, so have a set of stain removers on standby just in case.

Rugs

If you can manage it, clean rugs by shaking them outdoors. If you have a balcony, hang them over it and beat them with a traditional bamboo beater (a lightweight frying pan also works well). This cleaning method is often more effective than using a vacuum cleaner, and airing the rug in the sunshine will also remove odors and kill dust mites. It also uses less energy, saves on vacuum bags and exercises your arms!

WALLS

Marks on painted walls can all be cleaned with a damp soapy cloth, unless the walls have a traditional lime whitewash. This, if wiped, can cause the mark to smudge. Because lime whitewash is cheap and eco-friendly, the easiest way to clean these walls is to simply paint over any marks.

Dirt and grease on ceramic tiles in kitchens and bathrooms can be washed clean with a wet rag or

LIVING NATURALLY

Creating a healthy home (or a clean carpet at least!)

• Vacuum weekly with a high-efficiency cleaner. If you have kids, make that twice a week.
• Make your home a shoe-free zone. Remove your shoes and you'll reduce harmful house dust by up to 90 percent.
• Buy a coir door mat. Clean it weekly by taking it outside and banging it against the front wall. Don't deposit the dust over edible plants, since it may contain lead and other toxins.
• Replace bare concrete outdoors with flower beds. These will help to absorb dust and pollution.
• Wash your hands before preparing or eating food. Kids always seem to have dirty hands and a quick wash before snacking should be an obligatory routine in a healthy home.
• Don't smoke. That includes cigarettes, smoky fires and poorly maintained gas appliances. Yes, open fires are not healthy at all and are an inefficient way of heating your home.
• Avoid cleaners that contain toxic chemicals (see chart on page 165).

sponge and some washing soda, a product derived from sodium carbonate that is relatively safe, cheap and readily available. Mold grows if you don't dry tiles after they get wet, and washing with soda solutions will help to limit their growth. Make sure that corners and junctions are properly sealed using water-based acrylic sealants to prevent water from damaging your building materials.

OTHER SURFACES

Water is nature's best solvent and most nongreasy dirt will dissolve or be washed away by a good douse of warm water. In many instances, simply wetting surfaces and containers and leaving them to soak will help to remove hard deposits. Grease doesn't dissolve in water, so you will still need to buy soaps and other cleaners to clean things properly.

Cleaning
products

While common household cleaning products have all passed various health and safety tests, many have been manufactured using dangerous industrial processes and are still not completely free of toxins. Chlorine and phosphate, two ingredients found in many common household cleaning products, pose particular threats: they create serious water pollution downstream from our drains and are toxic when they come in contact with our skin. The eco-alternative is to clean your home with gentle and readily available products such as soap, soda, salt, warm water and some good old-fashioned elbow grease.

KITCHEN CLEANLINESS
Food needs to be kept and prepared in a clean environment where chances of bacterial contamination are low. By their very nature, kitchens are also home to the toughest cleaning jobs, with grease, oils and fats finding their way onto floors, work surfaces and ovens. But this doesn't mean you have to employ harsh cleaners containing toxic ingredients for the job. In fact, these products are just as likely to cause ill health as the bacteria they are designed to destroy.

You can clean most kitchen surfaces with soapy water and a little washing soda. A solution of washing soda or bicarbonate of soda, sponged down with clean water, will do the job for fridges and ceramic tiles, while diluted vinegar cleans glass and descales kettles. Squeezing a little lemon juice onto a cloth, rubbing this into the stain, then wiping clean removes most stubborn stains and heat marks on metal and melamine worktops.

Keep ovens clean by putting tops over your casserole dishes. Once you have finished cooking, coat the wet, greasy range surface with bicarbonate of soda and salt to make it easy to clean the next time. Sprinkle borax powder in your garbage can to get rid of odors.

Shiny metal surfaces
These have become a popular look in kitchens in recent years, but they involve a great deal of   >

< appreciating tarnish
Developing an eye for this beauty rather than the gleam of constantly polished silver or copper is one way to reduce pollution caused by the production and use of metal-cleaning products.

HARMFUL HOUSEHOLD PRODUCTS AND THEIR ALTERNATIVES

We all aim to have homes that are clean and safe sanctuaries, but many common household products contain proven physical and environmental toxins, which can accumulate over time and cause serious damage to our health. Take a good look in your cleaning cabinets and replace these with the suggested alternatives.

Household products	Harmful ingredient	Alternatives
Batteries	Cadmium, mercury, nickel, sulphuric acid, zinc	Use rechargeable batteries or mains power.
Bleach	Chlorine	Avoid bleaching or use hydrogen peroxide.
Carpets	Butadiene, styrene, ethylbenzene	Choose natural rugs and avoid cheap foam underlays.
Dyes	Ammonia	Use natural vegetable dyes.
Deodorants	Ethylene glycol	Use talcum powder.
Dry cleaning/ fabric cleaner/ spot remover	Perchloroethylene	Avoid dry-cleaning fabrics.
Lawn treatment products	Chlorothanol	Hand pull weeds and plant chamomile instead of grass.
Mothballs	Napthalene, paradichlorobenzene	Use lavender and cedar wood as repellents and keep closets closed.
Air fresheners	Paradichlorobenzene	Avoid creating smoky atmospheres, ventilate rooms well and perfume with fresh-cut flowers from your garden.
Cleaners, polishers	Methyl ethylketone	Use beeswax or a half white vinegar, half vegetable oil mixture.
Household plastics	Polyvinyl chloride	Use linoleum for floors and simple plastics such as polypropylene for containers.
Toilet cleaner	Hydrochloric acid	Use white vinegar, lemon juice, baking soda, borax, washing soda, hydrogen peroxide.

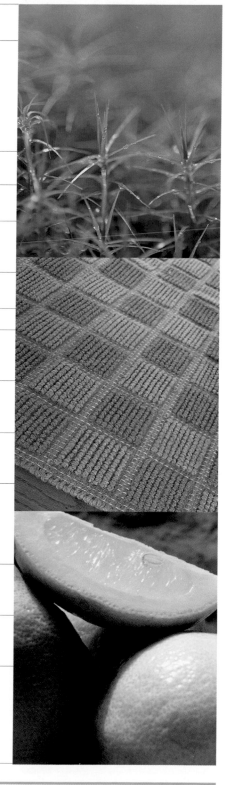

> cleaning to maintain them. The strong chemicals in metal polishes are also toxic and it is possible to overpolish metal surfaces to the point of destruction. Instead, adopt the traditional Japanese approach of refraining from maintaining the newness of metal and allowing the layers of tarnish to slowly develop into their own rich patina.

If you still prefer the polished look, use homemade products instead of store-bought ones. To clean gold metals, mix equal measures of vinegar and baking soda in a jar and polish well. Use bicarbonate of soda powder with a little water to polish chrome objects and simmer silver items in a pot of water with aluminum foil and a tablespoon of washing soda.

Dishwashing liquids
The standard commercial dishwashing liquid is usually

phosphate based, but the best eco-alternative is a vegetable-oil-based detergent with salt and plant extracts. Ecover is just one organization that makes alternative household products, dishwashing liquids included, which contain only botanical and natural ingredients. Buy them in bulk and reuse the containers for storing your own homemade house-cleaning fluids. The other benefit of using vegetable-based dishwashing liquids is that dirty sink water can then be filtered and used to water the garden either directly or via a buried trickle hose. Alternatively, use dirty water to soak pots and pans overnight.

Dishwashers
Older dishwashers use around 13 gallons of water and therefore waste power and water. Modern energy-efficient ones can cope with twelve place settings (two to three days' washing), use less than 5 gallons of water (the best use less than 4 gallons), recycle heat between cycles and use only air to dry the dishes. Minimize the energy required by modern

< saving water
A standard kitchen sink holds between 2½ and 5 gallons of water and washing dishes after a family meal usually involves between 5 and 8 gallons of water. An energy efficient-dishwasher uses less.

dishwashers by supplying hot water direct from your central water heater, filling the machine to its full capacity and using economy cycles. You can also save water by not using the prewash cycle: just dip dishes in a bowl of cold water after eating and this will stop deposits from drying in the first place.

If you don't have a dishwasher, then wash dishes in one bowl and rinse plates together in a second bowl of cold water. Leave pots to soak overnight with salt or potato peelings and wash them out with the next day's batch. Don't rinse

ECO-TIP

Dry cleaning alternatives
The active ingredient in dry cleaning, perchloroethylene, is a carcinogen that causes reproductive, developmental and environmental damage, so it's best to avoid buying clothes that need dry cleaning. In fact, many clothes labeled "dry clean only" can actually be washed by hand; clothes manufacturers find it cheaper to write this on the label than to test their clothing for washability. Consult a specialist cleaner, who will be able to give you more detailed advice on clothes labeled "dry clean only."

REMOVING STUBBORN STAINS

The active ingredients required to remove stubborn stains can be found in a number of common household products, so treat clothes with these before washing instead of buying specific, heavy-duty chemical products.

Stain	Method
Blood	Soak in cold water.
Coffee and tea	Soak in solution of warm water and borax.
Grass	Rub with glycerine.
Ink	Rub with milk for fountain ink, turpentine for ball-point ink.
Perspiration	Rub with clear vinegar.
Tar	Rub with eucalyptus oil.

under running water, since this will waste buckets of water (literally!).

WASHING CLOTHES

TV ads implore us to wash our linens "whiter than white." But white never stays white for long, and you could be forgiven for thinking that detergent manufacturers encourage this behavior for more than purely aesthetic reasons.

Apart from the environmental pollution caused by bleaches and other whiteners, there are plenty of good reasons to choose clothes that stay clean longer. The most

obvious is the pleasure of not having to wash, dry and iron clothes every other day.

Most outer clothing stays clean for far longer than you imagine and sometimes all it needs is a night on the line to remove the odors from yesterday's smoky bar.

General dirt can easily be removed from clothes using a combination of two parts soap flakes and one part bicarbonate of soda in a warm-water wash cycle on your washing machine. Stubborn stains may need to be treated beforehand (see chart above). An alternative method is

to use ionizing tablets that remove dirt in a washing machine without the use of conventional detergents. Ionizing tablets (or laundry disks) don't leave clothes smelling like "fresh daisies" but they do clean well and only need recharging every sixty washes. You'll still need to use hot water on white clothing and treat stubborn stains beforehand but you'll save money, reduce the number of trips to the supermarket and have detergent-free cleaning that's gentle to sensitive skin.

Waste management

Cleaning and maintenance can create a huge amount of garbage, and manufacturers, stores and city governments are all realizing that waste is, well, a waste. Even so, we still seem to be filling garbage bins at an inordinate rate, throwing out nearly a ton of garbage from our homes each year.

While we all still produce waste, many environmental designers now believe that the future will truly be waste free. Instead of producing waste, we will hand on our unwanted resources to recycling companies. We'll bundle them up at home to help the recycling companies, who'll pick them up, clean them and sell them back to manufacturers as raw material. Plastics will go back to the bag man, metals to the can-maker, glass to the bottle company and much of the rest will be composted for our garden centers or burned to produce heat and power. Recycling companies will be high-tech rag-and-bone men, and the old saying "where there's muck there's brass," will never be truer.

In order to make this happen, we householders will have to learn to reduce waste to a minimum, reuse as much as possible and then choose things that can be easily recycled at the end of their lives.

RECYCLING

To promote recycling of household waste, buy products that have packaging that is easy to reassemble. It is far easier to recycle a simple cardboard box, for example, than a plastic-coated metal can. Don't buy products that are packaged in complex containers, such as aerosols, air fresheners or oven cleaners, because more money goes into the can than into the product inside (it is even more of a waste when homemade products can do these jobs just as well).

You should also avoid buying dangerous and toxic products that will pollute the planet when discarded. If you can't avoid them, make sure that you dispose of them responsibly.

Set up a recycling closet at home. Old cards, paper and magazines can be used to soak up spills, given to the kids for painting and scrapbook making, or composted with garden and kitchen waste. Clean glass and

recycling
Paper, glass, metal and some plastics can all be reused easily, so always recycle products made from these materials. Ask your local council for recycling containers and pick up points in your neighborhood.

down any sharp burrs. In fact, most sensibly designed containers can be reused for years before they wear down and have to be thrown out.

Composting

Kitchen waste comprises 20 percent of household rubbish and can be composted and used as a free and effective fertilizer for your garden. You can make a compost area by putting a wire fence around a small corner of your yard or by buying a fixed or rotating compost bin from your local DIY store. Fill it with kitchen waste and garden cuttings and, in a few months, a rich mix of healthy garden food will appear.

To get good compost, layer dry material such as twigs between moist kitchen waste, add grass clippings to improve nitrogen content and insulate the pile with pieces of old carpet. Water occasionally to keep the area moist. Avoid adding animal or dairy fats, because these decompose very slowly, encourage the growth of flies and attract scavenging animals into your garden. Once the waste has composted, spread it onto your garden as a mulch and let worms do the job of mixing the nutrients into the soil.

Wormeries

Compost bins can also be converted into wormeries. These produce a richer liquid garden fertilizer that can kick-start new

plant growth without the need for chemical phosphates. To make a worm bin, take a standard plastic composter and drill holes on the sides about 4 inches from the bottom. Fill the bottom with gravel and water until it reaches the holes. Add kitchen waste, some manure and egg shells together with a handful of tiger worms (obtainable from an angling shop), then keep adding waste. The worms will multiply quickly and turn the compost into a very rich solution that you can mix with soil to produce excellent potting compost.

DISPOSING SAFELY

Quite a lot of our household waste is toxic and therefore needs to be disposed of carefully. Many cities have facilities for handling toxic household waste and you should call your local authority to find out more. Save up old oils, paints and pesticides and dispose of them through your region's hazardous waste service. You can cut up unwanted leather and other textiles and use them as rags or give them to charities. Take old medicines to your pharmacist for safe disposal.

Some products cannot be recycled so consider this when shopping. Disposable batteries, for example, add to waste fills, so always buy rechargeables or plug electrical items into outlets in your home.

plastic bottles and containers are good for mixing homemade cleaning products or for storing dried garden herbs. Cut plastic bottles in half and use them to protect growing plants in the garden. Cans and other metal containers can be recycled into paint pots but make sure you file

Household pests

Not only do our homes provide a living environment for humans, they also attract a myriad of creepy crawlies. While some pests cause only mild irritation, others carry diseases and can turn our homes into a complete misery. There are plenty of commercial products on the market that claim to kill with just one quick spray, but this is because they are full of noxious substances that are also harmful to humans. Instead, make your home pest free with simple physical barriers or natural pest repellents.

MOSQUITOES

Mosquito repellents, whether in sprays, coils or electric-socket tabs, contain DEET, a chemical that is toxic not only to mosquitoes but also to humans. While their use can be justified during a short trip to a hot climate, prolonged use is dangerous and unnecessary, especially when you can take alternative precautions.

In warm weather, mosquitoes can overwhelm the home, accounting for sleepless nights and itchy skin. In hot countries, mosquito screens across windows are almost obligatory and it is possible to make or buy similar screens in cooler regions. Where mosquitoes carry malaria, you should also use ceiling fans to stir the air, keep your skin covered, scent the air with citronella and use mosquito nets over beds at night. To reduce the number of mosquitoes in your garden remove all areas of still water, make sure your pond is aerated (a fountain helps to break up the water surface, where larvae grow) and keep it well stocked with fish and frogs that eat growing larvae.

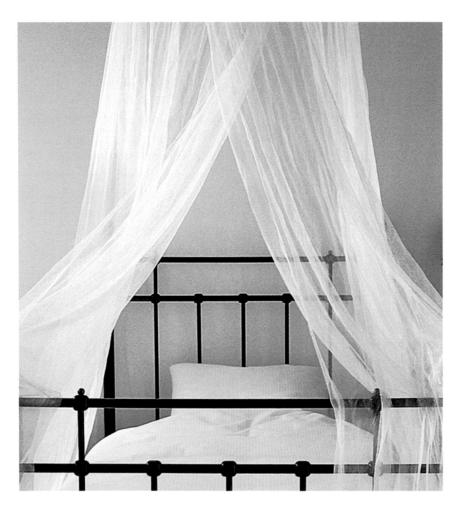

∧ **sleep well**
If you live in a hot and humid climate, mosquito nets are a necessity and a much healthier alternative to air conditioning and mosquito coils. Ceiling fans and open windows with insect-proof screens will help to create or let in cooling breezes.

MOTHS AND FLIES

These common visitors can often be found crawling around our closets and kitchen cabinets, where they lay larvae that chomp their way through natural fibers and food stores.

Moths

Napthalene and paradichloro-benzene are the active ingredients in mothballs and both are environmental toxins that alter natural ecosystems and destroy the balance between living creatures. Instead, control moths by keeping drawers, closets and kitchen cabinets closed and regularly air the contents to check for signs of moth infestation.

Flies

Bluebottle and house flies are pests that are attracted to your home by rotting food and open food containers. Instead of reaching for the standard fly spray that, although an effective killer, contains harmful chemicals and artificial perfumes that are neither healthy nor naturally biodegradable, avoid infestation in the first place. You can do this by covering food, clearing away leftovers right away and generally keeping kitchens and dining rooms clean. Grow and dry fresh herbs in and around your home to scent the air and repel flies. Keep trash bins clean and site them as far from your home as possible.

FLEAS, ANTS AND COCKROACHES

Ants and roaches are attracted by open food, so again it is important to keep your kitchen clean. Sprinkle some boric acid (available from hardware stores) along ant trails to stop the path being reused, and kill roaches by mixing equal parts of sugar and baking soda in a dish and placing this out of inquisitive children's reach. To prevent flea infestations, feed your pet tablets of brewer's yeast and garlic and bathe it regularly during the flea season. You can also sprinkle your pet's bedding with fennel seeds and rosemary, since the scent of these helps to keep fleas at bay.

RODENTS

Rats and mice gnaw through unprotected wood, electrical wiring and plastic plumbing and find homes in crevices inside your walls or under the floor. If you suffer from rat or mouse infestation, you need to close up any escape routes, such as holes in floorboards or skirting. While solid walls provide some protection, the best prevention is to store food and waste in sealed containers and to keep all surfaces free of food crumbs. If you keep a compost bin in the kitchen, make sure it has a secure lid to prevent smells from enticing vermin. Keep outdoor compost heaps away from the house and use a covered plastic or wood compost container rather than an open-sided affair.

If keeping your kitchen clean doesn't do the trick, then lay down humane traps (boxes with a one-way entry and a piece of food to entice rodents to enter) or get a cat to do the dirty work. Rat poison is a potential poison for small children, and the standard spring-loaded death trap only adds to the chance of contracting infection from rotting corpses hidden behind cabinets or under stairs. Rodents are also deterred by the strong scent of mint, so leaving sachets of mint leaves in your kitchen cabinets will also help.

7Eco-rating guide

This final chapter provides an eco-rating for many of the materials and elements you are likely to find around your home, from the surfaces you stand on and lean against to the furniture you lounge on, and how you use water and energy in your home. You will discover which are best suited to which areas of your home, for your health, for ease of maintenance and for the benefit of the planet. The ratings are as follows: 1 is excellent, 2 is average and 3 is poor; the lower the overall eco-score, the better the material or product. We have even taken price into account, so that saving the planet doesn't have to put a hole in your pocket.

Category	Energy consumption	Durability	Recyclability	Environmental pollution	Installation cost	Maintenance cost	Overall eco-score	Comments	Suitability
	Eco-friendliness							Comments	Suitability
Subfloor									
solid wood	1	1	1	1	2	2	8	Use local woods managed sustainably. Look for Forest Stewardship Council (FSC) certification. Protect from moisture. Can be used without further covering.	In wet rooms, protect with water-resistant covering.
concrete	3	1	3	2	3	1	13	Avoid on upper floors because heavy weight must be supported by complex structures that are difficult to change. Seal with low-odor resins or cover with additional flooring. Use recycled aggregate (crushed concrete and stone) to reduce environmental impact.	Can help to reduce overheating in warm climates and will collect and store solar heat in cool climates.
Floor finishes									
Wood									
local hardwood	1	1	1	1	2	1	7	Good replacement for tropical hardwoods. Alder, ash, beech, birch, chestnut, elm, hickory, lime, maple and oak are all popular hardwoods.	Avoid in wet environments.
reclaimed wood	1	1	1	1	2	1	7	Reclaimed parquet is often cheap and in good condition. Wider planks are more expensive. Good types to use include mahogany or maple parquet, and old oak or pitch pine boards.	Avoid in wet environments.
tropical hardwood	2	1	1	2	2	1	9	Only use woods with FSC certification.	Some woods, such as teak and greenheart, can be used in wet environments.
local softwood	1	2	2	1	1	2	9	Often cheap and plentiful, although less durable than many hardwoods. Good examples include pine, cedar, fir, larch and spruce.	

Category	Energy consumption	Durability	Recyclability	Environmental pollution	Installation cost	Maintenance cost	Overall eco-score	Comments	Suitability
		Eco-friendliness							
bamboo plywood	1	2	2	1	2	1	9	Not strictly a wood, but preferable to other tropical plywood.	Can be used in bathrooms.
nontropical plywood	2	2	2	2	1	2	11	Not as hard-wearing as solid wood. Choose plywood with low-odor resin content. Will need many coats of varnish to protect from damage.	Avoid in heavily used areas of the home and those that are likely to get wet frequently.
Soft flooring									
linoleum	2	1	2	1	1	1	8	This soft, warm and low-cost flooring is made from all-natural ingredients and is available in plain and marbled finishes.	Good for all types of rooms.
cork	1	2	2	1	1	2	9	This is made from natural materials, bound with glues and baked to form tough tiles. Seal to avoid pitting.	Suitable for less frequently used rooms, such as the bathroom.
rubber	2	1	2	2	2	1	10	Made mostly from synthetic materials, rubber is mixed with ground stones and binders to make a long-lasting, water-resistant material that can be dyed many colors. Some manufacturers use recycled or natural materials.	Use in rooms that get wet often, such as bathrooms, kitchens and utility rooms.
vinyl (PVC)	1	2	2	3	1	2	11	This is made from a complex mix of PVC binders and plasticizers, which have known carcinogenic contents. Softer vinyls give off more pungent odors than harder tiles.	Avoid or use only sparingly in rooms that get wet.
Hard flooring									
stone (slate, marble, granite, etc.)	2	1	2	2	3	1	11	Strong and low maintenance, but expensive. Choose locally produced stones in preference to imported stock.	Use sparingly in rooms that are heavily trafficked or get wet frequently.

Category	Energy consumption	Durability	Recyclability	Environmental pollution	Installation cost	Maintenance cost	Overall eco-score	Comments	Suitability
			Eco-friendliness					Comments	Suitability
reconstituted stone	2	1	3	2	3	1	12	Made from ground stone and cement or resins. It has a lower environmental impact than raw stone because it uses waste products efficiently.	Use sparingly in wet environments and heavily trafficked areas.
ceramic	2	1	3	2	3	1	12	Made from glazed or unglazed fired clay that can be colored with a variety of finishes.	Use sparingly in wet environments and heavily trafficked areas.
terrazzo	2	1	3	2	3	1	12	This mix of marble or glass is tough and long lasting. If laid on site, sealants are unnecessary.	Use sparingly in wet environments and heavily trafficked areas.
brick	3	2	2	2	2	2	13	If possible, use reclaimed bricks to reduce energy consumption and lime mortar to allow easier recycling in the future.	Use in external or semi-external situations.
metal flooring	3	2	1	2	3	2	13	Metal tile floors (including those made from aluminum and zinc) require a lot of energy for their production.	Avoid use if possible.
Floor coverings									
wool rugs	1	2	2	2	2	2	11	The more knots per inch, the tougher (and more expensive) they will be. Persian and Oriental rugs are particularly long lasting.	Well-made rugs can be used throughout the home, but don't use in areas that are damp or have a lot of traffic.
cotton rugs	2	3	3	2	1	2	13	Lighter and less hard-wearing than wool rugs. Most cotton is farmed irresponsibly so look for organic sources if possible.	Cotton is easily washable so it is suitable for use as mats in bathrooms.
fitted wool carpets	2	3	2	1	2	3	13	These are softer and more expensive than synthetic carpets.	A no-shoes policy in the house will increase a carpet's life and reduce cleaning costs.

Category	Energy consumption	Durability	Recyclability	Environmental pollution	Installation cost	Maintenance cost	Overall eco-score	Comments	Suitability
			Eco-friendliness						
natural fibers (sea grass, jute, sisal, hessian, etc.)	3	2	1	2	2	2	12	These are generally less processed than carpets and use less-intensive dyes.	They wear easily, so avoid in heavily trafficked areas.
fitted synthetic carpets	2	3	3	2	1	3	14	Nylon, acrylic and polypropylene carpets are not soft or hard-wearing but are cheaper than wool ones.	Avoid use when possible.
Carpet underlays									
felt	1	2	1	1	1	2	8	Ensure that this has adequate bounce to protect carpet from wear.	
recycled rubber	1	2	2	1	1	2	9	This has good eco-credentials, reducing carpet wear and noise transmission.	
sponge rubber	2	3	2	3	1	2	13	Many of these contain harmful organic chemicals and some are so soft that they crumble away after a few years.	
Internal walls									
wood stud and plaster-board	1	1	3	1	1	1	8	These are simple to construct and modify. Include cellulose insulation to increase sound insulation.	Suitable for all internal walls.
concrete block and plaster	2	1	2	2	1	1	9	Lightweight concrete blocks consume relatively little energy, but concrete walls are difficult to modify at a later date. To improve eco-credentials, use blocks made from waste materials, such as power-station ash.	Only use on floors that have been designed to take the weight of concrete.
brick and plaster	3	1	2	2	1	1	10	Brick is heavier and more energy intensive than lightweight concrete.	Avoid when possible.

Category	Energy consumption	Durability	Recyclability	Environmental pollution	Installation cost	Maintenance cost	Overall eco-score	Comments	Suitability
			Eco-friendliness					Comments	Suitability
Wall finishes									
wallpaper	1	2	2	1	1	2	9	A cheap and effective wall covering. Avoid vinyl wallpaper because it doesn't allow the structure to breathe.	Avoid in wet rooms.
wood paneling	1	1	2	1	2	2	9	Use FSC-certified softwood paneling.	Avoid in wet rooms to prevent rot.
cork	1	1	2	1	2	2	9	Cork tiles are tough and eco-friendly but can look dark and outdated.	Use in bathrooms or on walls used for posters or notes.
natural fibers	1	2	2	1	2	3	11	Paper coated with hessian, silk, wood veneers or dried grasses is less robust than printed paper but more interesting.	Use decoratively in living rooms and bedrooms.
ceramic tiles	3	1	3	2	2	1	12	Long lasting, water resistant and available in many styles, sizes and colors.	Use in bathrooms, kitchens, utility rooms and hallways.
metal paneling	3	1	1	3	3	2	13	Easier to fix than ceramic tiles but less resistant to water damage.	Avoid or use sparingly in place of ceramic tiles.
Natural paints									
mineral	1	1	1	1	2	1	7	Based on water glass (potassium silicate), this bonds deeply with plaster or concrete to create a long-lasting and colorfast finish.	Generally used on exterior plaster but can also be used for interior solid color and glazed finishes.
casein	1	2	1	1	2	2	9	This is distemper with the addition of a milk protein binder to make it tougher and longer lasting.	Can be used throughout the home.

Category	Eco-friendliness							Comments	Suitability
	Energy consumption	Durability	Recyclability	Environmental pollution	Installation cost	Maintenance cost	Overall eco-score		
distemper	1	3	1	1	1	2	9	This is made from chalk, water and glue mixed together and colored with natural pigments to create a grainy and soft surface that breathes well and glows in reflected light.	Suitable for plaster and woodwork that is far away from moisture and dirty hands.
Synthetic paints									
acrylic	2	2	3	2	1	2	12	Choose ones with low volatile organic compounds (VOC) to reduce environmental damage.	Can be used throughout the home, but natural paints are better.
high-sheen water based	2	1	3	3	2	2	13	These give off VOCs that cause physical damage over a long period of time.	Use on woodwork or metalwork, but avoid indoors.
oil-based	3	1	3	3	3	1	14	Same as high-sheen water-based paints, but with greater concentration of VOCs.	Use on woodwork or metalwork, but avoid indoors.
lead-based	3	1	3	3	2	2	14	Take care when stripping old paint that may contain lead.	Lead is a toxin and should be avoided in the home.
Furniture									
wood	1	1	2	1	2	2	9	Solid wood furniture is tough and long lasting. Choose local hardwood timbers with solid joints and waxed surfaces.	Avoid using in rooms that get wet easily because wood eventually rots.
plastic	2	2	3	2	1	2	12	Cheap, but often poorly made. UPVC in particular ages poorly, especially when exposed to the sun.	If well made, it will be tough, so use outdoors or for children's furniture.
metal	3	1	1	3	3	2	13	Steel and aluminum are commonly used to make chair frames and cabinets. If well made, they last a long time, but thinner metals often deteriorate quicker. Use recycled metals where possible.	Use sparingly around the home. Aluminum makes long-lasting garden furniture.

Category	Eco-friendliness							Comments	Suitability
	Energy consumption	Durability	Recyclability	Environmental pollution	Installation cost	Maintenance cost	Overall eco-score		
MDF and melamine	1	3	3	2	1	3	13	Cheap but short-lived materials that are best avoided unless designed carefully.	Avoid using in wet and fragile environments.
Lighting									
daylight	1	1		1	1	1	5	Enhance with light-colored surfaces. Reduce associated nighttime heat loss with curtains, aluminum blinds and high-efficiency double glazing.	Promote daylight by opening curtains and turning off electric lights.
compact fluorescent	1	1	3	1	2	1	9	A wide variety of sizes and qualities available, varying from dull, insipid color rendering and slow start to fast, small and mellow output.	Use for desk lamps and in ceiling shades. Choose warm color rendering and instant-on bulbs for living spaces, and cheaper bulbs elsewhere.
linear fluorescent	1	1	3	1	2	1	9	Slim-line tubes are most efficient. Choose electronic ballast type for instant on and nonflicker effect.	Use in bathrooms, in utility rooms and concealed above work surfaces in kitchens.
tungsten halogen	2	2	3	2	1	2	12	Small, punchy white light from low-voltage lamps with transformers.	Good for spot lighting in kitchens and living rooms. Can also be used in appropriate desk lamps.
tungsten	3	3	3	3	1	3	16	Short lived; high energy consumers.	Use sparingly with dimmer switches.
Ventilation									
passive stack ventilation	1	1		1	3	1	7	These small (4 to 6 inch) tubes with humidity-controlled dampers are good alternatives to positive extract ventilation.	Only use in bathrooms and kitchens where there is easy access to the roof directly above the room.
passive ventilators	2	1		2	1	1	7	Simple but not particularly energy conscious.	Use in living rooms and bedrooms.

Category	Energy consumption	Durability	Recyclability	Environmental pollution	Installation cost	Maintenance cost	Overall eco-score	Comments	Suitability
	Eco-friendliness							Comments	Suitability
whole-house heat recovery ventilation system	1	2		1	3	2	9	Relatively expensive but, if well designed with low-energy fans and good controls, will reduce heating energy in well-sealed homes.	Often only appropriate in modern houses with tightly sealed windows. Consult a supplier for suitability.
positive extract ventilation	2	2		2	2	2	10	Choose quiet and efficient fans and use humidity controls.	Use in kitchens, bathrooms and utility rooms.
Electrical energy supply									
renewable utility company	1			1	2		4	These charge around 15 percent above standard cost and a number of utility companies offer renewable energy.	Easy to convert your home without any modifications.
photovoltaic panels	1			1	3		5	Currently expensive and only produce electricity during daylight hours. Good potential provided system cost is reduced.	Suitable for south-facing facades only. Best suited to sunny climates.
wind turbines	1			1	3	1	6	Large-scale wind turbines are more efficient.	Expensive. Only suitable in remote locations with wind speeds of 15 mph or more.
standard utility company	3			3	1		7	These use traditional power stations that are energy intensive and wasteful.	Avoid using when possible.
Water conservation									
showers	1	1		1	1	1	5	Showers use only two-fifths of the water used in a bath. Avoid power showers.	

Category	Energy consumption	Durability	Recyclability	Environmental pollution	Installation cost	Maintenance cost	Overall eco-score	Comments	Suitability
			Eco-friendliness						
spray taps	1	1		1	1	1	5	Can be retrofitted to standard taps (which is unattractive), or new spray taps can be installed when upgrading.	Use in bathroom or kitchen sinks.
rainwater collecting system	1	1		1	2	1	6	Collecting rainwater for gardening is easy but collecting for washing and use in toilets requires significant investment.	
dual flush toilets	2	1		2	1	1	7	These can save at least half of the water used in traditional toilets.	
composting toilets	1	1		1	3	2	8	If you are not connected to the main sewer line, these can be cheaper than adding a septic system.	
gray water recycling systems	1	2		1	3	2	9	Recycling bathwater for flushing toilets or for gardening is relatively expensive but can be justified in new buildings.	
Heating/energy conservation									
heating controls and thermostats	1	1		1	1	1	5	Choose an internal thermostat and set it to below 70°F. Use a seven-day timer clock.	
water tank and pipes	1	1		1	1	1	5	Insulate with thick rock wool jacket and cork pipe insulation.	
attic insulation	1	1		1	1	1	5	600 feet of attic insulation is cheap to install and will reduce heat loss considerably.	
floor insulation	1	1		1	1	1	5	Necessary in older homes with wood floors. If possible insulate between floor joists and seal behind skirting boards.	

Category	Energy consumption	Durability	Recyclability	Environmental pollution	Installation cost	Maintenance cost	Overall eco-score	Comments	Suitability
	Eco-friendliness								
window and door weather-proofing	1	1		2	1	1	6	Reduces heating bills in winter. Seal over letter boxes on doors, too.	
curtains	1	2		1	1	1	6	These should be interlined and drawn in the evening.	
condensing gas boiler	1	2		1	2	1	7	If you are upgrading, choose a high-efficiency condensing boiler to minimize running costs and pollution. Not generally available in the U.S.	
secondary glazing	1	1		2	1	2	7	Use glass with low-emissivity (low-e) film to reduce heat loss even further.	Use if your single-glazed windows are in good condition.
wood stove	2	1		1	2	2	8		Only suitable in the country with good local wood.
draft lobbies	2	1		2	2	1	8	If you have the space, lobbies on front and back doors will help to keep heat in and dust out.	
low-e double glazing	2	1		1	2	2	8	Only slightly more expensive than traditional glazing. Worth the extra cost.	Good for living rooms and cold or shaded elevations.
wall insulation	2	1		2	2	1	8	Sensible option for cavity walls, particularly in windy and wet locations.	
solar thermal panels connected to solar water heater	1	2		1	3	2	9	Expensive but environmentally sound way of heating water.	Only sensible to install solar thermal panels once you have undertaken other improvements to your home.

Useful contact details

Updates and more detailed information is available on ecofriendlyhome.com
For any queries please email on info@ecofriendlyhome.com

Eco-organizations

Forest Stewardship Council
Washington, D.C.
International organization promoting sustainable forest management
(877) 372-5646
www.fscus.org

Friends of the Earth
Washington, D.C.
Environmental advocacy group
(877) 843-8687
www.foe.org

Greenpeace
Washington, D.C.
Environmental charity
(800) 326-0959
www.greenpeace.org

Green Seal
Washington, D.C.
Identifies and promotes products and services that protect the environment and conserve resources and habitats
(202) 872-6400
www.greenseal.org

International Federation of Organic Agriculture Movements
Tholey-Theley, Germany
Worldwide umbrella organization of the organic agriculture movement
(49) 6853-919890
www.ifoam.org

National Arbor Day Foundation
Nebraska City, Nebraska
Tree-care and conservation organization
(402) 474-5655
www.arborday.org

Organic Farming and Research Foundation
Santa Cruz, California
Promotes adoption of organic farming
(831) 426-6606
www.ofrf.org

Renewable Energy Policy Project—Center for Renewable Energy and Sustainable Technology
Washington, D.C.
Promotes renewable energy and provides information on renewable energy, energy efficiency and sustainable living
(202) 293-2898
www.crest.org

World Wildlife Fund
International organization supporting nature and the environment
(800) 960-0993 or (800) 225-5993
www.wwf.org

Eco-design

Center for Resourceful Building Technology
Missoula, Montana
Promotes environmentally responsible practices in construction
(406) 549-7678
www.crbt.org

Energy and Environmental Building Association
Bloomington, Minnesota
Promotes energy-efficient, environmentally responsible buildings and communities
(952) 881-1098
www.eeba.org

The Energy Outlet
Eugene, Oregon
Promotes electrical energy conservation in homes
(541) 683-5060
energyoutlet.com

Healthy Home Designs
Mill Valley, California
Environmentally responsible architecture
(415) 383-5105
www.healthyhomedesigns.com

Renewable energy companies

Atlantic Renewable Energy Corporation
Richmond, Virginia
Operates renewable energy projects
(804) 965-9530
www.atlantic-renewable.com

Green-e Renewable Electricity Certification
San Francisco, California
Administered by the Center for Resource Solutions; allows consumers to quickly identify environmentally superior electricity products in competitive markets
(888) 634-7336
www.green-e.org

Green Mountain Energy
Austin, Texas
Retail renewable power available in several states
(800) 286-5856
www.greenmountain.com

The Source for Renewable Energy
On-line index of renewable energy businesses
energy.sourceguides.com

Recycling organizations

Architectural Salvage, W.D. Inc.
Louisville, Kentucky
Reclaimed building materials
(502) 589-0670
www.architecturalsalvage.com

RecycleNet Corporation
Richfield Springs, New York
Provides information on secondary or recyclable commodities, by-products, used and surplus items or materials, and operates a trading Web site
(519) 767-2913
www.recycle.net

Urban Ore
Berkeley, California
Reclaimed building materials
(510) 559-4460
urbanore.citysearch.com

Government and trade associations

Center of Excellence for Sustainable Development
Washington, D.C.
A program of the U.S. Department of Energy providing information and services to help communities adopt sustainable development practices
www.sustainable.doe.gov

Energy Efficiency and Renewable Energy
Merrifield, Virginia
A program of the U.S. Department of Energy
that develops and deploys efficient and
clean energy technologies that meet the
energy needs of the United States, enhance
the environment and strengthen national
competitiveness; provides advice regarding
energy usage
(800) 363-3732
www.eren.doe.gov

Energy Star
Voluntary, U.S. government-led labeling
program for energy-efficient products,
including new homes, residential cooling and
heating systems, appliances, lighting and
electronics such as computers
(888) 782-7937
www.energystar.gov

National Association of Home Builders
Research Center
Upper Marlboro, Maryland
Conducts research on the design and
construction of homes and on issues such as
affordable and sustainable housing, the
environment and special-needs housing;
provides information to the home-building
industry
(800) 638-8556
www.nahbrc.org

National Fenestration Rating Council
Silver Spring, Maryland
Measures and compares the energy
performance of window, door, and skylight
products
(301) 589-6372
www.nfrc.org

Solar Energy International
Carbondale, Colorado
Provides advice and education regarding the
use of renewable energy sources
(970) 963-8855
www.solarenergy.org

General eco-merchants

Building for Health
Carbondale, Colorado
Environmentally responsible building
materials and home appliances
(800) 292-4838
www.buildingforhealth.com

Carlisle Restoration Lumber
Stoddard, New Hampshire
Floors made from reclaimed antique woods
(800) 595-9663
www.wideplankflooring.com

Carrier
Farmington, Connecticut, and Syracuse, New
York
Manufactures high-efficiency heating and
cooling systems, including a condensing boiler
(800) 227-7437
www.residential.carrier.com

Gazoontite.com
Retail stores and on-line catalog offering
products and information related to asthma,
allergies and better breathing
(800) 469-6673
www.gazoontite.com

Herman Miller, Inc.
Retail stores and on-line catalog offering
environmentally responsible office furniture,
including a 100-percent recyclable chair
Zeeland, Michigan
(888) 443-4357
www.hermanmiller.com

The Old House Parts Co.
Kennebunk, Maine
Reclaimed architectural and building materials
(207) 985-1999
www.oldhouseparts.com

NorthWest Builders Network
Eugene, Oregon
On-line resource for general building
information and products, plus information
on environmentally responsible building
practices and materials; includes builders'
environmental guide and an "enviro store"
(541) 895-5061
www.nwbuildnet.com

Real Goods
Hopland, California
Retail stores and on-line catalog featuring
ecologically responsible products for healthy
homes and lifestyles
(800) 762-7325
www.realgoods.com

Weather-Bos
Environmentally safe paints and finishes
(800) 664-3978
www.weatherbos.com

Other useful contacts

American Water Works Association—
Partnership for Safe Water
Denver, Colorado, and Washington, D.C.
Promotes safe public drinking water
(303) 794-7711 or (202) 628-8303
www.awwa.org

Environmental Building News (published by
BuildingGreen, Inc.)
Brattleboro, Vermont
Promotes environmentally conscious building
practices
(802) 257-7300
www.buildinggreen.com

Natural Home Magazine
Loveland, Colorado
Promotes environmentally conscious home
design
(970) 669-7672

Portfolio 21 (Progressive Investment
Management)
Portland, Oregon
No-load mutual fund focusing on companies
with a proven commitment to a sustainable
future
(877) 351-4115, ext. 21
www.portfolio21.com

Index

Picture credits

t= top, l=left, r=right, b=bottom, c= centre, cb=centre below, ca=centre above, mp=main picture. EWA=www.elizabethwhiting.com

2/3 IKEA; 4 The Holding Company; 5t Bhs:
5c Christy; 5b Bhs; 6mp Dave Young; 6bl
Elgin & Hall Ltd; 6bc General Electric
Mazda; 6br Solar Century; 8/9 Ed
Reeve/Living Etc/IPC Syndication; 9 Elgin &
Hall Ltd; 10 Gettyone Stone; 11t Solar
Century; 11b Images Colour Library;   13
Dave Young; 14t STOKKE FABRIKKER AS;
14c Elgin & Hall Ltd; 14b General Electric
Mazda; 15t David Murray; 15b Image Bank;
16mp The Timber Decking Association; 16bl
The Velux Company Ltd; 16bc English
Hurdle; 16br Prêt à Vivre; 18 Jeremy
Cockayne/Arcaid; 19t Cuprinol; 19c
International; 19b Laura Ashley; 20/21
NEXT Home; 21 English Hurdle; 22 Laura
Ashley; 23 The Velux Company Ltd; 24 Paul
Smoothy; 25 Simon Kenny /Belle/Arcaid; 27
Chris Gascoigne/View; 28t General Electric
Mazda; 28c Jam; 28b Ocean; 29 Jon
Boucher/ EWA; 30 Nolte; 32 Neil
Lorimer/EWA; 33t The Timber Decking
Association; 33b Rodney Hyett/EWA; 34
Gettyone Stone; 35 David Murray; 36
Homebase; 37 Elgin & Hall Ltd; 39t Prêt à
Vivre; 39b Klóber UK; 41 Austroflamm; 42
Tommy Candler/ EWA; 43l Peter
Woloszynski/ EWA; 43r Neil Lorimer/EWA;
44 Rodney Hyett/ EWA; 45l Nedra
Westwater/EWA; 45r Sake Powell/EWA;
46/47 Rodney Hyett/EWA; 47
International; 48tl Prêt à Vivre; 48tr
Monkwell; 48ca International; 48cb Bhs;
48b Swish; 49t House; 49b Crown Paint;
50mp LASSCO Flooring; 50bl Kersaint
Cobb; 50bc Auro Organic Paint Supplies;
50br Descamps; 52t The Holding Company;
52bl Magnet; 52br Stone Age; 53 LASSCO
Flooring; 54/55 James Morris/Axiom; 56
LASSCO Flooring; 57 Natural Flooring
Direct; 58tl Roger Oates Design; 58tr
Roundel Design; 58bl Resin Building
Products Ltd; 58br McCord; 59
Bartholomew Conservatories; 60 The Rug

Company; 61t Image Bank; 61b Jim
Holmes/Axiom; 62t Kersaint Cobb; 62ca
Natural Flooring Direct; 62cb,b Kersaint
Cobb; 63 Kersaint Cobb; 64 Forbo-Nairn
Ltd; 65 Kersaint Cobb; 67 Auro Organic
Paint Supplies; 68 Crown Wallcoverings &
Home Furnishings; 69tl Stone Age; 69tr
McCord; 69bl Fired Earth; 69br Ariston; 70l
LASSCO Flooring; 70r Dalsouple; 71 Graham
Henderson/EWA; 72 Armitage Shanks; 73
Jim Holmes/Arcaid; 74 Futon Company;
74/75t Sanderson; 74/75b Magnet; 76t
Shaker; 76ca,cb House; 76b Lakeland
Limited; 78 Peter Cook/View; 79 Habitat;
80/81t Descamps; 80/81b Earth Tones
Collection; 81t Earth Tones Collection; 81b
House of Fraser; 82 Sanderson; 83 McCord;
84mp Vale Garden Houses Ltd; 84bl Marks
& Spencer Direct; 84bc Nolte; 84br Crown
Paint; 86t LimeStone Gallery; 87l Chris
Gascoigne/View; 87r Dennis Gilbert/View;
88t The Holding Company; 88b Elgin & Hall
Ltd; 89 Chris Drake/Living Etc/IPC
Syndication; 90 Ligne Roset; 90/1 Peter
Aprahamian/Living Etc/IPC Syndication;
92tl The Holding Company; 92tr Marks &
Spencer Direct; 92b Elgin & Hall Ltd; 93t
Cuprinol; 93b Wilman Interiors; 94 Elgin &
Hall Ltd; 95 Sanderson; 96t Ariston; 96b
Nolte; 96/97 Dennis Gilbert/View; 98
Shaker; 99t The Holding Company;
99bl,bc,br Magnet; 100 Magnet; 101
Stonell Ltd; 102 Peter Cook/View; 103t,c,b
Neff; 103r Marks & Spencer Direct; 104t
IKEA; 104b Elgin & Hall Ltd; 104/105 Peter
Cook/View; 105 Marks & Spencer Direct;
106 Magnet; 107tl Bhs; 108t Yves
Delorme; 108/109 Dennis Gilbert/View;
109t Marks & Spencer Direct; 109b Futon
Company; 110l Sanderson; 110r Futon
Company; 110/111 James Morris/Axiom;
112 Elgin & Hall Ltd; 113t Marks & Spencer
Direct; 113b Found; 114t Colourwash; 114b
Crown Paint; 114/115 Chris

Gascoigne/View; 116 Armitage Shanks;
117tl Magnet; 117tr House; 117bl LASSCO
R.B.K; 117br Marks & Spencer Direct; 118l
Dennis Gilbert/View; 118r Marks & Spencer
Direct; 119tl Magnet; 119bl G.E.C.
Anderson; 119br Armitage Shanks; 120l
Found; 120r Christy; 121tl Dalsouple;
121tr International; 121bl LimeStone
Gallery; 121br Armitage Shanks; 122t Wax
Lyrical; 122b Premium/Arcaid; 123 Ocean;
124 Elgin & Hall Ltd; 124/125 Ed
Reeve/Living Etc/IPC Syndication; 125br
JELD-WEN UK; 126t,c Ocean; 126b Found;
127 Elgin & Hall Ltd; 128t IKEA; 128b
Neff; 129 Forbo-Nairn Ltd; 130t Julie
Phipps/Arcaid; 130b Premium/Arcaid;
130/131 Julie Phipps/Arcaid; 132 The Velux
Company Ltd; 132/133 Dennis
Gilbert/View; 134t Vale Garden Houses Ltd;
134b Bartholomew Conservatories;
134/135,135 Vale Garden Houses Ltd;
136mp Gettyone Stone; 136bl,br The Stock
Market UK; 136bc IKEA; 138 Gettyone
Stone; 139t,c Construction Resources;
139b Elgin & Hall Ltd; 140t IKEA;
140bl,bc,br Found; 141 STOKKE FABRIKKER
AS; 142 Telegraph Colour Library; 143t The
Velux Company Ltd; 143b Boots; 144 The
Stock Market UK; 145t Ocean; 145b
Gettyone Stone; 146 Gettyone Stone; 147
The Stock Market UK; 148 Images Colour
Library; 149t JELD-WEN UK; 149b smart
car; 150 Gettyone Stone; 151t Karl-
Dietrich Buhler/EWA; 151b The Stock
Market UK; 152/153 Image Bank; 153
Grand Illusions; 154bl,bc David Murray;
156 Image Bank; 159 David Murray; 160
David Murray; 162t Dyson; 162b Gettyone
Stone; 163 Kersaint Cobb; 164 David
Murray; 165c House of Fraser; 166 Image
Bank; 168/169t Gettyone Stone; 168/169b
Telegraph Colour Library; 170 IKEA.

Carroll & Brown would particularly like to thank the following companies for supplying invaluable information and images:

Ariston
Armitage Shanks
Auro Organic Paint Supplies
Austroflamm
Bartholomew
Bhs
Boots
Christy
Colourwash
Construction Resources
Crown Paint
Crown Wallcoverings & Home Furnishings
Cuprinol
Dalsouple
Descamps
Dyson
Earth Tones Collection
Elgin & Hall Ltd
English Hurdle
Fired Earth

Forbo-Nairn Ltd
Found
Futon Company
G.E.C. Anderson
General Electric Mazda
Grand Illusions
Habitat
The Holding Company
Homebase
House
House of Fraser
IKEA
International
Jam
JELD-WEN UK
Kersaint Cobb
Klóber Limited
Lakeland Limited
LASSCO Flooring/LASSCO R.B.K
Laura Ashley
Ligne Roset
LimeStone Gallery
Magnet
Marks & Spencer Direct
McCord

Monkwell
Natural Flooring Direct
Neff
NEXT Home
Nolte
Ocean
Prêt à Vivre
Resin Building Products Ltd
Roger Oates Design
Roundel Design
Sanderson
Shaker
smart car
Solar Century
STOKKE FABRIKKER AS Norway
Stone Age
Stonell Ltd
Swish
The Timber Decking Association
Vale Garden Houses Ltd
The Velux Company Ltd
Wax Lyrical
Wilman Interiors
Yves Delorme

Acknowledgments

Author Acknowledgments

Thanks to all my friends and family for putting up with my passion, my work colleagues for helping me organize my life when time was tight, my old friend Rachel Aris who commissioned this book, and my editor Madeleine Jennings for her advice, patience and friendly bonhomie.

AMERICAN EDITION

Publisher James Connolly

Editorial Director Floyd Yearout

Americanization Editor Karen O'Donnell Stein

Production ImageComp

Proofreader Sarah Pirch

BRITISH EDITION

Project Editor Madeleine Jennings
Designer Vimit Punater

Deputy Art Director Tracy Timson

Photographers Jules Selmes, David Murray

IT management Elisa Merino, Paul Stradling
Production manager Karol Davies

Picture researchers Clare Carter, Sandra Schneider, Richard Soar
Proofreader Clare Hacking
Index Madeleine Jennings

Thanks also to Simon Daley for original design and Vimit Punater for technical illustrations